Move to Cambodi

Move to Cambodia

A guide to living and working in the Kingdom of Wonder

LINA GOLDBERG

IMAGINARY SHAPES   NORTH ADAMS, MASSACHUSETTS

Move to Cambodia
A guide to living and working
in the Kingdom of Wonder

by Lina Goldberg

movetocambodia.com

Published December 2012 by Imaginary Shapes

Book design by Imaginary Shapes
imaginaryshapes.com

ISBN 978-0-9883224-1-7

For more about moving to and living in Cambodia,
including our regularly updated blog about what's
happening in the Kingdom of Wonder, visit us at
movetocambodia.com.

Contents

Welcome to Cambodia: An Overview   I

Get to know Khmer culture   6
     Saying hello and good-bye   II
     Cambodian courtesy   I2
     Face   I3
     Corruption and bribes   I5
     Bargaining   I6
     Food   I9
     Religion   2I
     Weddings   23
     Festivals and holidays   25
Currency   28
Climate and weather   30
     Cool season   30
     Hot season   3I
     Rainy season   32
     When to visit Cambodia   33

Planning Your Move to Cambodia   35

Why move to Cambodia?   36
Cambodian visas   38
     Applying for a Cambodian visa   39
     Extending or overstaying your Cambodian visa   4I
International movers   43
Vaccinations   45
     Where to get vaccinated in Cambodia   47
Cost of living   48
     Costs of basic items in Cambodia   48
Budgeting for your move   5I

Living in Cambodia   55

Where to live in Cambodia   57

Phnom Penh   57

Siem Reap   60

Battambang   64

Sihanoukville   64

Kep and Kampot   66

The Cambodian provinces   67

Homes and apartments   69

Long-term hotels and guesthouses   70

Finding a shared apartment   70

Finding your own apartment   72

Buying property in Cambodia   74

Utilities   75

Hiring household staff   79

What to do when you first arrive   82

How to get a phone and SIM card   82

Banking   85

Mail   87

Transportation   92

Getting around by tuk tuk   92

Getting around by moto taxi   95

Driving and traffic   97

Long-distance buses   102

Flights   104

Religious organizations and worship   107

Love and family   111

Sex and dating   111

Gay culture   113

Expat kids in Cambodia   116

Health and medical care   120

Common ailments   120

The state of medical care   122

Hospitals   123

Doctors and clinics 124

Pharmacies and medicine 125

Women's health 126

Dental care 129

Eye care 130

Health insurance and travel insurance 131

Getting medical care outside of Cambodia 134

Safety and security 137

Robberies and bag-snatchings 137

Hotel and apartment break-ins 139

Emergency numbers and dealing with the police 140

Recreational drugs in Cambodia 141

Advice for women 144

Clothing and dress 145

Women and safety 146

Working in Cambodia 149

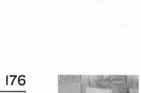

Employment in Cambodia 150

Work permits 151

Finding work 153

Doing business in Cambodia 156

Starting a business 158

Running a business 160

Teaching English 164

Finding work as an English teacher 166

Taxes 168

Volunteering in Cambodia 170

Resources: For More Information 176

Web resources 177

Suggested reading 184

Part one

Welcome to Cambodia: An Overview

They don't call it the Kingdom of Wonder for nothing!

The Kingdom of Cambodia is often referred to by lazy travel writers as a "study in contradictions." And as so often in this beautiful country, the lazy way works just fine. Cambodia is indeed filled with great contrasts, between rich and poor, countryside and city, beauty and squalor, friendliness and rudeness, heat and. . . well, wet heat. But those who get to know the country will likely find that, taken all together, the contradictions of Cambodia add up to something uniquely wonderful.

Indeed, Cambodia is known as the Kingdom of Wonder and attracts more than two million international visitors each year. As more and more Westerners discover Cambodia as a great place to visit, not a few have found that it's also a great place to live and work. The country's thriving expat community attests to the many attractions Cambodia

City of Temples

(Opposite) Bas relief carving at the temples of Angkor

I

Year-round summer

Sunrise on Koh Thmei

Planted in the tropics

Palm trees on Koh Russei, or Bamboo Island

holds for ambitious professionals, creative types, and lotus-eating beachcombers.

The low cost of living, the year-round summer weather, the friendly people, and a wealth of employment opportunities are among the many reasons foreigners have chosen to make a permanent move to Cambodia. Moreover, the red tape involved in living here and getting a job is easily dealt with, compared to most other countries. No wonder so many expats have found that the Kingdom of Wonder is the place where they can make their dreams come true.

Cambodia is planted firmly in the tropics, located between Thailand, Laos, Vietnam, and a 443-kilometer coastline along the Gulf of Thailand (think beaches). The weather is always warm, although there are monsoons for parts of the year. The country is about twice the size of Portugal — 181,035 square kilometers (69,898 square

Tropical wonderland

Island life on Koh Totang

miles) — and divided into 24 provinces. The most populous city is Phnom Penh, which is also the capital and home to most of Cambodia's expats.

Despite the government's best efforts to destroy or sell off Cambodia's natural beauty, the country still has jungle rainforests, tropical islands, lush rice paddies, and temperate forests. The Tonle Sap and Mekong River are the heart and soul of Cambodia, providing food and employment for many Khmers.

Cambodia has a long and tumultuous history. Sandwiched between Thailand and Vietnam, Cambodia has been pushed and pulled between them for centuries, with the more recent French and US interventions causing additional devastation. The United States' secret war in Cambodia between 1969 and 1973 killed tens of thousands and displaced hundreds of thousands more, setting the stage for the 1975 takeover by the communist Khmer

Rouge. Its attempt to forcibly transform the country into an agrarian cooperative resulted in the deaths of millions in the course of the Khmer Rouge's four-year rule. The country is still struggling to recover from the ravages of its recent history.

Today the Kingdom of Cambodia is a constitutional monarchy whose strong-man prime minister, Hun Sen, has held power since 1985, while the present monarch, King Norodom Sihamoni, was only installed in 2004. Under Hun Sen's leadership, Cambodia has become a developing country that's constructing more infrastructure with each passing day. There's a large emerging middle class and a stratum of "Khmer riche" whom you'll see aggressively driving Land Rovers and Lexuses around the city streets. However, Cambodia is also still a very poor country, even when compared to many of its neighbors in Southeast Asia. In 2010 the per capita annual income was $2,470, and 25.8 percent of the population was living below the poverty line. The divide between rich and poor in Cambodia is extreme, and corruption is endemic.

The population is nearly 15 million, most of whom are Khmer, although there are substantial Vietnamese and Chinese populations as well. There are also many French, Japanese, Korean, Australian, American, British, and European expats. The main language spoken is Khmer. Older Cambodians who were educated before Cambodia got its independence from France in 1953 often speak French. English, at varying proficiencies, is also widely spoken, and most young people have studied at least a little bit of English. Luckily for English speakers, there are a lot of young people: 50 percent of the country is under the age of 25.

Cambodia's official religion is Theravada Buddhism, which 95 percent of the population practices some form of. Most Cambodians are fairly relaxed when it comes to religion, although they greatly respect the many saffron-clad monks you'll see going in and out of the thousands of pagodas around the country. During some of the major holidays and festivals, outsiders can participate in or observe some of the ceremonies.

There's much more to learn about Cambodia and its many wonders, and no better way to learn than by living here. Whether you've just begun daydreaming about making a move or already have your plane ticket, we've pulled together just about everything you need to know.

A young country

Children are everywhere in Cambodia, where half the population is under 25.

Get to know Khmer culture

Spending any time in Cambodia is to experience a world whose values, etiquette, and traditions are very different from those in the West.

Particularly if you're planning to relocate here, your life will be infinitely easier if you make the effort to learn at least a bit about Cambodia's history and about Khmer culture and religion.

Understanding the concept of face certainly helps, especially when it comes to dealing with corruption and bribes. You'll also need to learn how to correctly execute the *sampeah*, the Cambodian way of saying hello and good-bye, as well as how to bargain. And of course you'll want to know a bit about Cambodian food.

Then there are the celebrations. Cambodia has dozens of holidays and festivals every year, and we've got information on the most important ones. Even if you have no plans to get married in Cambodia, you need to know about the country's nuptial rituals. It's a rare expat who doesn't get invited to a Cambodian wedding or three, so best to know what you're getting yourself into!

Cambodia's history

Any discussion of Khmer culture and modern Cambodia must begin with a look at the country's troubled past.

What is now Cambodia was an ancient civilization, starting as early as 4200 BCE (Before the Common Era). Pots from that time have been found in northeast Cambodia and are similar to ones you'll find today in Phnom Penh's Orussey Market. Then came the Funan Kingdom and then the Chenla Kingdom. Next was the golden age of Cambodian civilization: the Khmer Empire.

Between the 9th and 13th centuries the Khmer Empire was one of the most powerful forces in Southeast Asia, ruling parts of modern-day Thailand, Burma, Laos, and Vietnam. The Khmer Empire's capital city was Angkor; what remains of its temples is now a major tourist attraction outside of Siem Reap.

It is believed that water supply problems hastened the end of the Angkorian monarchy, and the final straw was when the Thais captured Angkor in 1431, spurring Khmer migration toward the Phnom Penh area. From 1500 until the arrival of the French in 1863, Cambodia was pushed and pulled between its now more powerful neighbors, the Vietnamese and the Thais. During this time Cambodia suffered great territorial losses and was nearly swallowed up altogether.

In 1863 King Norodom signed an agreement with the French making his country a protectorate of France and bringing baguettes to the Kingdom. Like most of Asia, Cambodia was occupied by the Japanese during World War II, but France's German-collaborating Vichy government was still nominally in charge until the Japanese briefly took complete control in 1945. After the war the French regained control again, but in 1953 they agreed to grant Cambodia its independence.

During the 1950s and 1960s, while war raged in neighboring Vietnam, King Sihanouk gave lip service to neutrality, while at the same providing tacit support for the North Vietnamese. By the mid-1960s the North Vietnamese were setting up bases in Cambodia's eastern provinces and using the port of Sihanoukville for supplies in their war against South Vietnam and the United States. In 1969 the US began a bombing campaign in Cambodia that lasted until 1973, dropping 2.7 million tons of bombs — around the same amount as dropped by the Allies in Europe during World War II. Hundreds of thousands of Cambodians were killed or displaced.

In 1970 King Sihanouk was overthrown by a new government headed by the US-backed Lon Nol. Sihanouk fled to Beijing and threw his support to the fledgling Cambodian communist group, the Khmer Rouge, who vowed to overthrow Lon Nol.

Sihanouk's support encouraged many Cambodians who knew little about communism to join the ranks of the Khmer Rouge, and a bloody civil war soon began. Later that year the United States and South Vietnam invaded Cambodia in order to destroy North Vietnamese bases. However, the North Vietnamese had already retreated deeper into the Cambodian countryside and begun to aid the communist insurgency. Many believe that it was the United States' Southeast Asian intervention, and in particular its massive bombing campaign, that allowed the Khmer Rouge to gain credibility and drove many Cambodians to join their ranks.

Between 1970 and 1975 the fighting between the Lon Nol regime on one side and the North Vietnamese and Khmer Rouge on the other was brutal, leaving hundreds of thousands of Cambodians dead. On April 17, 1975, the Lon Nol government collapsed and the Khmer Rouge, with a Paris-educated intellectual named Pol Pot at the helm, took over and renamed the country Democratic Kampuchea.

Within days the Khmer Rouge evacuated Phnom Penh in a radical attempt to restructure Cambodian society. The cities were forcibly emptied and nearly the entire Cambodian population was forced to work as slave laborers in the countryside, where the supposedly more ideologically "pure" peasants were put in charge. The goal was to turn

Cambodia into an agrarian, communist society with no religion, no intellectuals, and no currency. The result was one of the most violent and drastic deliberate upheavals ever inflicted on a society.

It did not take long before the Khmer Rouge regime turned on itself, going through a series of violent purges meant to weed out those who were not sufficiently dedicated to the cause. Many leaders of the Khmer Rouge defected to Vietnam, where they put together a government in exile.

In December 1978 the Vietnamese government invaded Cambodia, and by early 1979 Vietnam had liberated Cambodia from the Khmer Rouge and installed a government of its own choosing, made up largely of the Khmer Rouge defectors who'd fled to Vietnam and led by Hun Sen. By this time huge numbers of Cambodians were starving and hundreds of thousands had fled to refugee camps on the Thai border.

The Khmer Rouge were in power for less than four years, but during that time between one and three million Cambodians died, close to a quarter of the entire population. Many were executed by the Khmer Rouge, and many more died of starvation and disease. Those who survived had their families ripped apart, were forced to marry complete strangers, were stripped of their culture and religion, saw all their hopes destroyed, and suffered torments most of us can barely imagine.

Though out of power, the Khmer Rouge were still able to put up resistance to the new regime and fighting continued long after the Paris peace agreements were signed in 1991. As part of the agreement, the United Nations undertook to administer the country for two years, in one of the UN's most ambitious and expensive plans ever. The UN Transitional Authority in Cambodia (UNTAC) was hailed as a success by some and derided as a boondoggle by others. Nevertheless,

Cambodia did manage to hold elections in 1993, with more than 90 percent of Cambodians casting votes.

Celebration of democracy proved premature, though. When the Cambodian People's Party (CPP), led by Hun Sen, did not win the election, the CPP threatened to lead a secession of Cambodia's eastern provinces. The country bowed to the CPP's threats and Hun Sen was made the second prime minister (royalist Norodom Ranariddh was the first).

Until this point the Khmer Rouge still had a seat in the UN and were recognized by many Western governments as the legitimate rulers of Cambodia. But after the 1993 elections they were exiled to fighting in the provinces (which is pretty much all they had been doing after 1979 anyway). The following year, 1994, they were outlawed. Defections to the government fractured the group until they eventually disintegrated and the last hardliners surrendered in the late 1990s.

In 1997 Hun Sen ousted his then coalition partner and co-prime minister in a military-backed coup. He's still in power today.

In 1998 Pol Pot died, never having faced justice for the atrocities committed by the Khmer Rouge under his leadership. That same year the CPP swept the Cambodian elections, as they have ever since. In the intervening years the country has taken small steps toward improvement, including agreeing to allow trials of the remaining top Khmer Rouge leaders by a UN-backed tribunal, a process that is still going on at the time of writing.

The almost three-decade-long war devastated the country, which lost most of its infrastructure, its cultural and educational institutions, and its intellectuals, who were either killed or fled the country. An entire generation of Cambodians was starved, tortured, and traumatized, and there are many who believe that this trauma has been passed down to the next generation. People often blame all of the country's ills on the Khmer Rouge period, which is a gross oversimplification of the country's difficult history. But there is no denying that this period had a profound effect on Cambodia's culture and people that will resonate for generations to come.

If you'd like to know more, we suggest you read up on Cambodia's history to better understand the country and its people. We've listed some of the best sources in the **Suggested reading** section (page 184).

Saying hello and good-bye

In Cambodia social interactions are usually governed by centuries-old traditions of respect and hierarchy that may not be immediately obvious to the average expat. This is evident every time Cambodians greet you or each other.

The traditional Cambodian way to say hello and good-bye is to place the hands together, with the palms touching (a posture Westerners often associate with praying), and bow the head. Similar to the Thai *wai*, this is called the *sampeah*, and it is how Cambodians greet one another, particularly for the first time. The formal greeting in Khmer is "*Choum reap sor*" and should be said while *sampeah*ing. (The more informal "*Susaday*" is reserved for casual situations and does not involve a *sampeah*.) "*Choum reap lear*" is the formal good-bye.

Where you place the *sampeah* in front of your body depends on the age and relationship of the person you are greeting. The higher your *sampeah*, and the lower your bow, the more respect you are showing.

When you greet people of the same age and social standing as yourself, put your hands together in front of your chest and bob your head. When you greet your boss, older people, or those to whom you would like to show respect, your *sampeah* should be positioned so that your fingertips are just below your mouth. Parents, older relatives, and teachers should be greeted with the *sampeah* at nose level. Eyebrow-level *sampeahs* are reserved for monks and the king, and forehead-level *sampeahs* are exclusively for prayer, sacred sites, and temple worship.

Many foreigners, in an attempt to be polite, over-enthusiastically *sampeah*, offering monk-level greetings to waitresses at local restaurants. This can actually be seen to cause a loss of face, so make sure you keep your *sampeahs* at appropriate levels. Traditionally, Cambodians do not *sampeah* to children, street vendors, and beggars; in these cases the polite response to a greeting is to do no more than nod and smile.

Cambodian courtesy

Some forms of Cambodian behavior that may seem somewhat rude to Westerners are in fact expressions of courtesy. For example, Cambodians will often ask you your age long before they get around to learning your name. They do this to determine whether you are older than they are, so they can greet and address you properly. Cambodians greet everyone with a title that conveys information about their relative age and social status. For example, a slightly older person will be called *"bong,"* which means older brother or sister.

Traditionally, Cambodians regard avoiding eye contact as a sign of respect, and they will only make eye contact with their social equals. Therefore, if someone avoids your eyes while greeting you, they aren't being rude, just respectful!

Expats should also know that it is not considered polite to touch a person of the opposite sex, and even friendly hugs among opposite-sex friends are avoided. (Same-sex friends, on the other hand, often walk hand in hand or otherwise display non-sexual affection.)

While many Cambodian men now shake hands when they meet, especially with Western men, most Cambodian women *sampeah*. Cambodian women will shy away from shaking hands, particularly with men, so it's important to return the *sampeah* properly. Not to do so is the same as not shaking a hand that's been extended to you for that purpose.

Face

Understanding the Asian concept of face is crucial for those planning on living and working in Cambodia. The dictionary definition of face is "Value or standing in the eyes of others; prestige." Face is dignity, honor, reputation, and social importance all rolled into one. In Cambodia, saving face and giving face are critical, and losing face is deplorable.

While you may think that face has nothing to do with you, foreigners often unintentionally cause locals to lose face, and then are confused by the extremely negative reaction they get. Relationships sour, business deals go awry, and expats put themselves in physical danger when the Khmer concept of face is misunderstood or disregarded.

Simply put, you cause someone to lose face by making them look foolish, stupid, or ill-informed, by damaging a relationship, or by losing your temper.

Situations in Cambodia should be handled far more diplomatically than they would be at home. For example, saying, "That's not right—here, let me show you" to one of your colleagues while others are present might be perfectly acceptable at home, but will likely be seen as loss of face for your colleague in Cambodia. (The best way to handle a situation like this is very diplomatically and while no one else can overhear.)

Cambodians will sometimes bend the truth, in matters great or small, and the cause of these small lies is frequently face. Khmers do not like to admit that they do not know something and so may make up an answer to save face, or will quickly blame someone else for their lack of knowledge. If you ask a question and get a blank stare in response, let the other person evade the issue as gracefully as possible; don't press the point and force them to admit they don't know the answer. Pointing out obvious lies won't help anything—it will cause them to lose face and will not be taken well.

In addition, losing your temper is considered a great loss of face, both to yourself and those around you. Anger is not well received, and if you lose your cool you'll see the Cambodians around you cringing in embarrassment or erupting in anxious laughter. Westerners whose angry outbursts are met with a chorus of giggles often just get angrier, but they're not being mocked. Rather, Cambodians often laugh or smile when they are nervous or uncomfortable.

Belittling Cambodians is ineffective and ill-advised—while it may make you feel better, it invariably makes the situation worse. Whenever possible, be diplomatic. Every situation should be negotiated so that both parties feel as if they have won. Do not say "no" directly when you can help it; try and smooth out the situation to make it seem that for anything you are gaining, you are giving something up as well. Be respectful to your elders. Be very mild in your criticism, and if you do need to give someone negative feedback, make sure it is not in front of others. Do your best to not embarrass anyone and they will do the same to you (sometimes to a fault).

Corruption and bribes

No talk of Cambodian culture would be complete without
mention of corruption, which has been the linchpin of
the country for centuries and is no less so today. This is,
inevitably, difficult for expats to understand and to manage.
Expats living in Cambodia often list corruption and bribes as
their number-one complaint about the country—and many
locals do, too.

Corruption is endemic in Cambodia, from teachers
demanding daily cash payments from their students to tax
officials offering to waive businesses' enormous tax bills in
exchange for large bribes. As an expat living in Cambodia
you'll no doubt be affected by the corruption that permeates
the fabric of life in the Kingdom, but happy are the expats
who learn not to let it impact their lives too severely.

Generally, people—both foreigners and Cambodians—are expected to make a small payment, often
referred to as "tea money," when they receive services or to
facilitate transactions. How much this bothers you can be a
matter of perspective.

For example, if you are the victim of a crime, you will
usually have to pay a small, unofficial fee to get a police
report for your insurance company. Many foreigners are
aghast at the idea of policemen asking for bribes. But
another way to look at it is as payment for services rendered.
In the West, policemen are usually funded through tax
revenue and are paid a living wage. In Cambodia most
residents, locals and expats alike, pay few or no taxes to
the government and policemen can make less than $40 per
month, not nearly enough to support a family. So paying a
few bucks when you need a police report or get pulled over
seems like a reasonable compromise.

That's not to say that corruption is warranted or that
bribery is okay—it's not. The culture of corruption in

Cambodia is compounded by the corruption in Cambodia. Because the government generates so little revenue through legitimate means (most revenue is siphoned off by corrupt police who don't give real tickets and corrupt tax officials who don't make anyone pay their bills), it can't afford to pay those police and officials enough to motivate them to not demand bribes. It's a vicious circle with no end in sight. Foreign aid, which comprises a solid half of Cambodia's GDP, is also susceptible to the endemic corruption (and some might say a cause of it).

Increasingly, though, foreign businesspeople are standing up to the culture of corruption in Cambodia and refusing to pay bribes to facilitate business transactions. Many businesspeople find that a Khmer friend or staff member is able to more easily argue against "facilitation fees" on their behalf than they can themselves. If you will be running a business in Cambodia, consider joining one of the business associations we list in the **Working in Cambodia** section (page 149).

It's up to you to decide whether or not you are willing to pay bribes in Cambodia. If you do, be aware that like everything else, they are open to negotiation.

Bargaining

Throughout Cambodia, bargaining is the norm for many transactions. So learning how to bargain is an important skill that all new expats should learn.

Khmers are not known for engaging in the kind of cut-throat bargaining you may have experienced in other countries. They may attempt to mark up a product by 20 to 100 percent, versus those other nationalities who ask for 1,000 percent of what they are hoping to eventually get. Price negotiations are usually very cordial in Cambodia and should result in smiles all around. The goal should not be to screw the seller to the wall and get them to accept the lowest possible price they can stand—that would entail a painful loss of face. Seek rather to find a price that seems fair to both of you. If you offer a price and your seller agrees, you will be expected to then buy the item, so do not negotiate unless you are ready to purchase.

However, it's important to know when *not* to try and bargain. Stores that have price tags are usually not willing to negotiate prices, and you'll look foolish if you try. Restaurants, including the smallest street food stands, do not bargain. Your visa fee is non-negotiable—although the "facilitation fee" you might be asked for if you cross at a land border usually is! Most other things, though, are bargainable.

Be aware that many sellers have three tiers of pricing: one for tourists, one for expats, and a third for locals. The easiest way to get the price down from the initial high starting point is to show that you aren't a tourist by being either a regular customer or speaking Khmer. The most important expression to know is *"T'lai na!"* ("So expensive!"). This, accompanied by a sharp intake of breath, as if you are physically pained by the exorbitance of the price, will usually result in an offer to accept a lower amount. Negotiating in riel rather than dollars and learning the numbers in Khmer so you can bargain in the local language are also helpful tactics.

The most important thing in learning to bargain well is to find out what the going rate of the product you are purchasing is. For example, the starting price of a T-shirt at Phnom Penh's Russian Market is usually $5 (about 20,000 riel), but sellers are generally willing to go down to 6,000 or 7,000 riel. If you offer them this price, they will take it, on the assumption that you know this is the going rate. However, had you started by offering 2,000 riel, they would have assumed that you were just an inexperienced backpacker

Endless variety

Mangos, pineapple, papaya, and watermelon are sold by mobile street vendors (left) and banh hoi, a Vietnamese-influenced dish made with rice vermicelli noodles is a popular noodle dish (right).

Fresh seafood

Crab from Kep served with young green pepper

and would still try to push for $2 or $3. The best way to find out the going rate of an item is to ask around. The expat forums and groups listed in the **Web resources** section (page 177) are good places to start.

Food

Cambodian food is perhaps the most overlooked of all Asian cuisines. Too often Cambodian cooking is dismissed as a lesser version of Thai or Vietnamese fare. Living in Cambodia will give you the chance to learn about this much misunderstood cuisine and enjoy its unique charms.

It's true that Cambodian food has much in common with that of its neighbors, particularly the cooking of Vietnam. Many dishes that are widely known as Vietnamese are also common in Cambodia. (Remember, part of southern Vietnam used to be part of Cambodia not so very long ago, and both countries have a shared history of colonization by the French.) For example, those tasty East-West sandwiches, called *banh mi* in Vietnam, are just as popular in Cambodia, where they are called *num pang pâté*. Other Cambodian dishes are more similar to Thai food, although Cambodian dishes usually contain less chili and less sugar, and coconut milk appears less often.

The most important part of every meal is rice. In fact, Cambodians greet each other by saying *"Nyam bai howie nov?"* ("Have you eaten rice yet?") At lunch and dinner in Cambodian homes each person is served a large bowl of rice. Then at least three or four other dishes, usually including a soup (*samlor*), are served family-style. *Prahok*, a pungent fermented fish paste, is used to flavor many dishes and for expats can take some getting used to. *Kroeung*, a distinctive spice paste made with a base of lemongrass and galangal, is the foundation of many Cambodian dishes. Freshwater fish from the Mekong and Tonle Sap make up a large part of the Cambodian diet, whether dried, processed into *prahok,* or cooked up in that famous Cambodian speciality, *amok.*

A typical Cambodian breakfast is rice porridge, called *bobor,* that's similar to Chinese congee. Rice and rice noodles figure heavily at the Cambodian breakfast table. A favorite way to start the day is *nom banh chok,* sometimes called the Cambodian national dish: rice noodles topped with a fish-based green curry gravy made with lemongrass, turmeric root, and kaffir lime. Another popular breakfast noodle preparation is *kuy teav,* a soup made from pork or beef bones and rice vermicelli and topped with fried shallots, green onions, and bean sprouts. *Bai sach chrouk,* or pork and rice, is one of Cambodia's simplest and most delicious breakfast options.

Snacking is a popular Cambodian pastime, particularly snacking on street food. If you're worried about getting sick, the safest street foods are those that are cooked in front of you and served hot, which kills off bacteria. Ice in Cambodia is also usually fine; it's specially made in ice factories.

You'll find different snacks available on Cambodia's streets at different times of the day. Early in the morning vendors offer breakfast dishes such as *kuy teav* and *bai sach chrouk* at small roadside stalls. In late morning through afternoon, roving vendors sell fresh cut-up fruit. Students crowd the streets late in the afternoon to enjoy such restoratives as spring rolls and barbecued beef skewers tucked into baguettes and topped with a green mango slaw.

Other street food favorites include iced coffee with sweetened condensed milk (*karfe toek doh koh toek gok*), fried noodles (*mi char*), chive cakes (*num kachay*), and paté sandwiches (*num pang pâté*). You'll find these dishes sold by roving vendors pushing carts around town and at small restaurants that set up shop on the sidewalk. For adventurous eaters, street food is a great way to learn about local fare while on a budget. On the street many delightful dishes usually cost no more than $1, far less than at Cambodia's Western restaurants.

For those who aren't convinced that they will like Cambodian food, there are hundreds of restaurants serving all types of international food in Cambodia. American, British, French, Italian, Korean, and Japanese expats have all set up restaurants serving their country's specialities, and that's not all. Those who are looking to follow a vegetarian, vegan, or halal diet will find many options. While local cuisine may be the least expensive choice, your favorite foreign comfort food won't be hard time come by, both in restaurants and supermarkets.

Religion

Theravada Buddhism is Cambodia's state religion and has been since the 13th century, except during the Khmer Rouge period. During that time, all monks were disrobed or killed and most religious scholars were murdered or fled into exile. Today the country is about 95 percent Buddhist. There are also two Muslim communities, the Cham and the Malay, making up 3 percent of the population. Just under 3 percent are Christians, plus there is a substantial population of Western missionaries trying to raise that figure. In the northeast of the country, many of the ethnic minority groups practice tribal religions.

Before Cambodia embraced Buddhism, there was Hinduism. Back in the day, Hinduism was one of the Khmer Empire's official religions. In fact, Angkor Wat is the largest Hindu temple in the world, and one of the only dedicated to Brahma. And while Hinduism is no longer directly practiced in Cambodia, it influences Khmer Buddhist practices, such as weddings, funerals, and the use of astrology to find auspicious dates for important events.

The Cambodian approach to Buddhism is the same as their approach to most things: relaxed. Most Cambodians visit the pagodas for the major Buddhist holidays, such as *Pchum Ben* (Ancestor's Day), and this is often the extent of their religious observances. Few Cambodians abstain from all of the Five Precepts of Buddhist belief, which prohibit killing, stealing, fornication, lying, and drinking. While they may not follow all of the rules, Cambodians still believe in reincarnation and the idea that one's position in life is derived from past actions. (This may explain why, as a rule, they treat their dogs so poorly.)

Most Cambodians identify as Buddhist, but their version of Buddhism includes forms of ancestor worship, shamanism, and animism that predate Buddhism. In almost all Cambodian homes (and even at the temples), you'll find spirit houses, small shrines to appease bad spirits and keep them away from the homes' residents. Most Cambodians, particularly in the provinces, believe in ghosts and spirits. There are myriad folk tales about sorcery and ghosts that many Khmers accept as fact. One such is the story of a half-ghost, half-girl who slips through the windows of houses after pulling out her internal organs and leaving her corpse outside. Khmers call this spirit *arb*, or *arb thmob*. Shamans are often consulted for illnesses which are believed to have been caused by evil spirits.

Unlike in most Christian religions, Buddhists who take vows to become a monk do not commit to this calling for life. It is common for Cambodian men to become monks for a short period of their life—usually a few weeks or a few months—to bring merit to their parents and to become closer to their Buddhist faith. This is usually done earlier in life, starting at age 13. The most common reason, though, that low-income Cambodians choose to become monks is to gain access to education that they might not be able to get otherwise. And for poor families in the provinces, having one less mouth to feed is a tempting proposition (long-term monkhood is much more common among Khmer youth from the countryside). Today less than 5 percent of men become monks, compared to 50 percent in the pre-Khmer Rouge days and close to 100 percent a century ago.

Older women, particularly widows, often choose to live at the pagodas as helpers so as not to be a burden on their families. Called *mae chi*, they shave their heads and eyebrows, clean and prepare the altars for ceremonies, and follow ten precepts (compared to the 235 that nuns used to keep).

There are also many Western religions and churches represented in Cambodia. See the **Religious organizations and worship** section (page 107) for more details.

Weddings

Weddings are important events in Cambodia. Rural Cambodians often use matchmakers and have arranged marriages, while city kids increasingly choose love matches. Premarital sex is considered unacceptable — for women, at least — and divorce, while easy to obtain, is uncommon. Most Khmer young people marry before the age of 25, and women often get married as teenagers.

A traditional wedding is a complicated and expensive affair that can go on for days, requiring multiple intricate outfits and lots of very early morning wake-up calls. A wedding usually lasts three days, with many different ceremonies relating to ancient mythical Khmer stories that are done in a specific order to join the bride and groom in matrimony. Some weddings can last a week while others are only a day long, determined usually by the wealth of the parties involved.

Even if you don't know any Cambodians when you first arrive, you'll find that you're often invited to weddings. Unlike Western weddings, where the guest lists are closely monitored, Cambodians will often invite all and sundry to their weddings, hoping to make the affair as large and impressive as possible. When foreigners are invited to weddings they are usually only invited to certain portions that are meant for an audience, or to the final evening celebration. In the cities, these are often held in large halls or on the street under a canopy.

If you're invited to a Khmer wedding, with your invitation you'll be given an envelope in which to put the cash gift you're expected to give the happy couple to help defray the wedding's enormous cost. Give according to your means; the average gift from a foreigner is around $20, but give more if the bride or groom is your employee or close friend. On entering the reception you may be surprised to find an eagle-eyed mother-in-law manning the reception table, writing down the names of all of the guests and the amount that they've given. It's not greed that dictates this behavior; rather, they want to make sure they know what the appropriate amount is to give when you invite them to your wedding later down the line.

Dress for guests is usually semi-formal. Men are fine in dress shirts, and skirts or dresses for women are acceptable. At weddings in the provinces, it's best to go with clothes that are conservative and do not show the shoulders, but in Phnom Penh, more revealing clothing is not uncommon. Women often wear traditional Cambodian dress to weddings, but this is not required.

Most weddings include a sit-down dinner and lots and lots of drinking. When drinking beer, Cambodians will clink glasses before every sip, saying, *"Chol muoy!"* There's also lots of dancing, which will include dances with steps that you don't know, but as the foreigner you will be good-naturedly forced to participate. If you're lucky, you may also be asked to be in some of the wedding photos, even if you've never met the bride or groom before. Although you might be tempted to demur, don't! Weddings are among the most pleasant insights into Cambodian culture available to expats, photographs and all.

Festivals and holidays

There's no shortage of holidays in Cambodia, with two dozen or more public holidays each year. In addition, other holidays, such as Chinese New Year, although not officially acknowledged, are widely celebrated nonetheless. The most significant Cambodian holidays are listed below.

Khmer New Year

Celebrated on April 13 or 14 each year, Khmer New Year, *Bon Chol Chhnam Thmei,* is a three-day affair that traditionally marks the end of the harvest season and is Cambodia's single most important holiday. The cities shut down for a week over Khmer New Year while Cambodians return to their home villages (often referred to by Cambodians as their homeland) to spend time with their families, have parties, and visit the local pagoda. Traditionally Cambodians considered themselves a year older every Khmer New Year rather than celebrating on their actual birthdate, although that is starting to change.

Pchum Ben

Another extremely important holiday in Cambodia is *Pchum Ben* (Ancestor's Day), a 15-day holiday that usually runs from the end of September to mid-October. During *Pchum Ben*, the spirits of dead ancestors are thought to be especially active, or they may even return to earth. Cambodians dress in white and bring food offerings to monks at the pagodas during this time; some believe that these offerings bring merit that indirectly benefits the departed ancestors, while others hold that these food offerings are transferred directly to the dead. During this holiday Cambodians spend a lot of time at the pagodas making offerings and praying for their ancestors.

Ancestor's Day

During *Pchum Ben*, Cambodians dress in white and bring offerings to the pagodas.

Water Festival

Every November the water in the Tonle Sap changes course and Cambodians gather in Siem Reap and Phnom Penh to celebrate the Water Festival, *Bon Om Touk*. Colorful boats race on the river and two million Cambodians descend on Phnom Penh to watch them. (Festivities in Siem Reap are similar, but not as enormous.) Water Festival is a chaotic time in the capital city, with hundreds of thousands of people coming in from the provinces to watch the races. In 2010 one of the worst stampedes in history took place during Water Festival on the bridge to Koh Pich, leaving 350 people dead.

Royal Ploughing Ceremony

Held to mark the start of the rice-growing season, the Royal Ploughing Ceremony, *Bon Chroat Preah Nongkoal*, usually takes place in May. During the observances, which are typically led by the king, sacred oxen plow a ceremonial row and are then presented with plates of food, most of which represent the crops of Cambodia. Based on which foods the oxen eat, the Royal Palace's soothsayer makes predictions for the season ahead. Wine is also offered to the oxen; if they imbibe, it portends disaster.

Currency

No worries about changing money — the US dollar is Cambodia's unofficial second currency.

The official currency in Cambodia, the Cambodian riel, trades at around 4,000 riel to the US dollar. But there's a 90 percent level of dollarization in the country. What this means is that you don't need to be concerned about getting riel when you arrive in Cambodia. In fact, the visa you get on arrival must be paid for in US dollars.

Most tourist-oriented businesses quote prices in dollars, as do most grocery stores in the larger cities. Small stores may quote prices in riel, but they will all accept dollars as payment. Unlike in many countries, if you pay in US dollars the exchange rate you will get is quite fair. At the time of writing the official exchange rate is 4,006 riel to the dollar, versus the street rate of 4,000 to the dollar, a difference of less than 1 cent.

Because they don't use American coins in Cambodia, you'll get change for your purchases in riel (1,000 riel is 25 cents). If you do want to change money so that you have riel on hand, you can do so at any bank in Cambodia. You'll get better rates in the local markets, where you'll be able to identify the moneychangers by their glass cases filled with piles of notes. Be warned, though, that it's rare to find notes over 10,000 or 20,000 riel ($2.50 and $5, respectively), so changing a relatively small amount of US dollars can leave you with a big pile of cash.

At border towns, such as Koh Kong or Ha Tien, you'll often find the currency of the neighboring country also in use, meaning there can be three currencies in circulation: the riel, the dollar, and the Thai baht or the Vietnamese dong.

In the Cambodian countryside the economy is almost entirely in riel, but even so you will always be able to use dollars in small denominations. Do not expect anyone to change a $20 bill for a $0.50 purchase, though, so plan ahead and have lots of $1 and $5 bills. Your US dollars will be rejected if they are ripped, torn, or otherwise overly abused (although you can expect to see filthy riel in circulation). Old-style US bills are also not welcome, so make sure that the cash you bring is fairly new. ATM machines in Cambodia dispense Cambodian riel and US dollars. However, if you are using a foreign ATM card, you will only be able to withdraw dollars.

Keeping it riel

The Cambodian riel only comes in small denominations, so have some US dollars handy, too.

Climate and weather

If you're not a fan of freezing, snowy winters, you're going to love Cambodia!

Cambodia is a tropical country — it's located just a smidge above the equator — with a usual temperature range of 21 to 35°C (69.8 to 95°F). Hot and steamy would be a good way to describe the weather here, but lest you find this unappealing, imagine walking around at night in a T-shirt without ever having to worry about bringing along a sweater. (Although that T-shirt may be covered in mango juice, since Cambodia's weather means cheap tropical fruit year round.) There's no harsh winter, and in fact no winter to speak of at all. Bring a sweater anyway, though, since many buses, offices, and stores like to keep the air-conditioning on high.

Cambodia is always warm (some say hot), with two distinct seasons, dry and monsoon (that is, rainy). Within those seasons, there are also cool and hot periods. The standard view is that Cambodia has three seasons: cool season, hot season, and rainy season.

Cool season

December–February

The weather starts to cool down in November and is actually pleasant in December and January. These are the months to visit if you want to be reminded of what a tropical paradise Cambodia is — the beach weather in Sihanoukville and the islands is perfect during this time of year. The temperature in Phnom Penh ranges from 21 to 32°C (70 to 90°F). When the thermometer dips to the low end of that range, it's not uncommon to see Khmers wearing parkas and complaining about how cold it is.

January is the coolest month of the year. February is still pleasant, but temperatures can start to rise by the end of the month. Because it has the best weather of the year, cool season is also when mobs of tourists descend on Cambodia. So for those who are sensitive to crowds, this is perhaps the least enjoyable time to travel around the country and especially to visit Angkor Wat, which is at its most mobbed during cool season. That said, cool season is also when Cambodia is at its most temperate, so for many it's still the best time to visit the temples or do any sort of hiking or trekking.

Hot season

March–June

April is usually the hottest month of the year, when temperatures start to climb to 40°C (104°F). It's called dry season, but the humidity makes it feel hotter than whatever the weather report says. During April and May in Cambodia the heat can accurately be described as oppressive. There's a serious dearth of shade, the air is still, and the streets are dusty. In parts of the country, slash-and-burn farming results in hazy skies. If you're considering living in Cambodia part-time, hot season is the season to avoid.

Many expats try to arrange to vacation abroad during hot season, so this is often when they make their yearly pilgrimage to their home countries. Expats who stay in Phnom Penh spend as much time as possible in or near the many pools the town has to offer, or drinking cocktails and complaining.

It rains occasionally during hot season, usually in short, powerful showers that are less than an hour long.

Rainy season (hot and cool)

June-September, October-November

Most expats dread their first monsoon season in Cambodia, but by the time they've slogged through the months of hot season, the rains come as a welcome respite. One of the most important things to remember is that although it can rain upwards of 20 days out of every month in rainy season, the showers are generally short (less than an hour) and predictable, usually happening in the afternoons.

Umbrellas are generally useless during monsoon season, as the rains are often accompanied by powerful winds. The most effective protection against rain is one of the 2,000-riel ($0.50) colorful plastic ponchos that can be found for sale all over the country. Plastic flip-flops, the footwear of choice for both expats and Cambodians, are also the most sensible rainwear. That's true even in the cities; both Phnom Penh and Siem Reap have experienced flooding during the last few rainy seasons, on a small and large scale respectively.

The upside of rainy season is that the rains every afternoon usually bring some relief from the high temperatures in July through September. In October and November it is still raining, but the temperatures start creeping down, with average highs of around 30°C (86°F) and lows around 23°C (73°F).

Rainy season is a great time to travel around Cambodia, as the country is mercifully empty of tourists.

When to visit Cambodia

Most of the year in Cambodia is lovely, but some times are nicer than others to visit.

For those who are sensitive to heat, cool season from November to February is the best time to visit Cambodia, specifically December and January. This is high season for the tourism industry in most of the country, and the popular destinations—Siem Reap, Sihanoukville, Kep, Kampot, and Phnom Penh—do most of their tourist business during this time. In particular, the Angkor Wat complex at Siem Reap is usually packed with visitors from all over the world.

Beach weather is perfect during this time of year, and you'd be advised to make a reservation in advance for accommodation in Sihanoukville and the Cambodian islands. During high season, rates in Sihanoukville are higher than during the rest of the year.

For those looking to save money and avoid the crowds, rainy season offers the opportunity to see the sights without having to fight for a spot at the Angkor Wat reflecting pool. Hotels, particularly in Sihanoukville, are often empty at this time of year, so this is when you'll find good deals. Photographers also prefer the light in the rainy season, when the sky is clear (compared to the smoky, dusty hot season) and the rice paddies are green and lush.

Rainy season

When it monsoons, Siem Reap often floods.

What's brewing

Kingdom is Cambodia's largest craft brewery.

Time to start planning

A weathered clock in
Battambang's Psar Nat

Part Two

Planning Your Move to Cambodia

Planning to relocate to a new country can be a time-consuming and stressful affair. Not so Cambodia.

There are lots of reasons to make the move to the Kingdom, not least of which are the country's relaxed approach to visas, its friendly locals, and its low cost of living. The weather is either a great reason to live here (you'll never experience winter again) or the one drawback (if you have trouble adjusting to tropical heat). And there's only one way to find out — move to Cambodia! Save up some money (we'll help you budget for your move), don't forget to make sure your vaccinations are in order, pack your bags, and hire the movers. We'll have a cold beer waiting for you when you arrive.

Why move to Cambodia?

There are many reasons to move to Cambodia. . . here are but a few.

Expatriates from all walks of life land in Cambodia for wildly different reasons. Some are after development jobs that will move their careers forward. Others are looking for a relaxed retirement. Still others are seeking a place where expenses are so low that they can afford to pursue creative endeavours without having to endure the hassle of working a traditional 9-to-5 job.

Despite their different backgrounds, foreigners can generally agree on a few reasons to settle here:

Getting a visa is easy. For less than a dollar a day, almost anyone can get a visa to stay in the country. Cambodia has one of the most relaxed visa programs in the world. . . for now.

The cost of living is low. Cambodia is cheap. Not as cheap as a lot of backpackers hope, but it's still very inexpensive to live here. Most expats can survive by working part-time, a luxury they would not have back home.

The weather. Okay, maybe most expats can't agree on this one, but anyone who has lived through a harsh, snowy winter can appreciate Cambodia's year-round warm temperatures. . . although most do agree that hot season can be unpleasant.

Cambodia is filled with great opportunities. Whether you're looking to get work experience in the development sector, teaching experience in the classroom, or material for your novel, Cambodia offers an abundance of opportunities for those willing to pursue them. Foreign experience is highly valued here, and most expats are able to find a job easily. In fact, many are able to find jobs that they wouldn't be regarded as qualified to do at home.

The locals are friendly. Serial expats know that in many countries settling in can be difficult due to difficult locals. Cambodians can be difficult, of course, but they're always friendly. If Thailand is known as the "land of smiles," Cambodia could be called the land of genuine smiles. Even small interactions like bargaining with a tuk tuk driver usually involve smiles and laughter. Male expats also find that their charms are magnified in Cambodia and that they are far more impressive to Khmer women than to the girls back home.

Life is easy. It's a mystery as to why, but expats in Cambodia just seem to have easier lives than they do in their home countries. Maybe it's because they're finally able to afford to have someone else clean their apartments, or just that they're working fewer hours, but foreigners who've settled in Cambodia fall in love with the country. They may whine and complain, but don't believe them. If they're here, they're having a good time.

Cambodian visas

For many potential expats, the easy visa situation in Cambodia is one thing that makes moving to the country so appealing.

You can get a long-term visa for Cambodia easily and renew it indefinitely without being sponsored by a company (or having any particular qualifications to do anything, in fact). This is certain to tighten up eventually, but for now Cambodia is one of the easiest countries in the world to emigrate to, visa-wise.

As a visitor to Cambodia, there are two types of visas available:

Cambodian tourist visa. The tourist visa (T class) is best for those who know they will be staying 30 days or less.

The 30-day tourist visa is available to travelers in advance or on arrival (for most nationalities) for a cost of $20. The tourist visa can be renewed once for an additional 30 days for a fee of $45. After that, tourist visa holders must leave Cambodia and come back and obtain a new visa. If you are planning on staying in Cambodia, don't bother with a tourist visa and start with an ordinary visa instead.

Cambodian "ordinary" visa. For anyone who is considering staying in Cambodia for an extended period of time, the ordinary visa (E class) is the best option. This visa used to be called the business visa but is now called the normal or ordinary visa. It is also valid for 30 days and costs $25. The difference between the ordinary visa and the tourist visa is that the ordinary one can be extended indefinitely.

Once you have your first 30-day ordinary visa for Cambodia, you can extend it from inside the country for 1, 3, 6, or 12 months. It's advisable to extend it for 6 or 12 months, as these visa types are multiple-entry. The 1- and 3-month ordinary visas are single-entry only, meaning that if you leave for a weekend trip to Vietnam, you'll need to get a new Cambodian visa when you return.

Applying for a Cambodian visa

What you need to apply for a visa to Cambodia

- A passport that is valid for at least another six months and has at least one blank page

- A passport-sized photo (if you don't have this, you can just pay a $2 fee)

Where to apply for a Cambodian visa

At the airport. If you're from most countries, you can get a visa on arrival at both of the Cambodian international airports, Phnom Penh and Siem Reap. You do not need to do anything in advance—you'll be given the paperwork on the plane and you just need to get in line on arrival with your passport photo, cash (in US dollars), and passport. There is an ATM at the airport in arrivals that dispenses US dollars if you don't have any on hand.

At a Cambodian embassy. If you prefer to get your visa in advance—or if you are from Afghanistan, Algeria, Bangladesh, Iran, Iraq, Nigeria, Pakistan, Saudi Arabia, Sri

PLANNING

Lanka, or Sudan—you'll need to visit the closest Cambodian embassy in your home country. (And if you are from one of those restricted countries, you'll need a return ticket and sponsor letter or letter of invitation from an employer or organization.)

At a land border crossing. You can also apply for a visa at the following Cambodia land border crossings:

Cambodia-Vietnam border

1. Bavet International checkpoint

2. Kha Orm Sam Nor International checkpoint

Cambodia-Thailand border

1. Cham Yeam International checkpoint

2. Poipet International checkpoint

3. O'Smach International checkpoint

This isn't recommended, though, as getting visas at land border crossings in Cambodia is generally a hassle, requiring numerous bribes and payments. It's best to get a visa in advance, before attempting a land crossing. If that's not possible, don't worry, but expect to pay between $1 and $20 in extra fees and bribes.

Online: the E-visa. One other option is the Cambodian E-visa, which can be obtained online. It is only available to citizens of the same countries for which visas on arrival are available (that is, everyone except citizens of Afghanistan, Algeria, Bangladesh, Iran, Iraq, Nigeria, Pakistan, Saudi Arabia, Sri Lanka, and Sudan), so there's really no benefit to using it. It is only offered for the tourist (T class) visa and costs an extra $5 on top of the regular visa fees, and it is only available to those entering Cambodia at the Siem Reap and Phnom Penh airports and the Bavet, Poipet, and Cham Yeam land border crossings. You can get your Cambodian E-visa online (www.mfaic.gov.kh/evisa/). The main reason to use an E-visa is to avoid scams at the land border crossings.

Extending or overstaying your Cambodian visa

Extending your Cambodian visa

If you have a 30-day tourist visa, you can extend it one time for an additional 30 days for a fee of $45. If you have an ordinary visa (E class) you can extend it for 1, 3, 6, or 12 months for between $45 and $300.

Currently, Cambodian visas cannot be renewed online.

Technically there's an official way to extend your visa by going to this address:

Department of Immigration
322 Russian Boulevard, opposite Phnom Penh Airport
Phnom Penh, Cambodia

Independence Monument

Celebrate your independence with one of the most relaxed visas in the world.

Everyone who's tried it this way recommends against it, though. The process can take ages, may require multiple bribes, and is just generally a pain.

The easy way to extend your Cambodia visa is to use any of the hundreds of local travel agents in town. They'll take care of the paperwork for you and it takes two business days.

You'll need:

- A passport that is valid for at least another six months

- A blank page in your passport

- One passport-sized photo

- Renewal fee in US dollars

- A 12-month, multiple-entry visa costs $265 to $300, depending on the fee added by the agent. The agent's fee is usually somewhat negotiable.

Overstaying your Cambodian visa

It's not advisable, but you can overstay your Cambodian visa at a cost of $5 a day for the first 30 days and $6 a day after that, payable at Immigration on your way out of the country.

If you plan to only stay a few days more than 30, this is often cheaper than getting a visa extension. However, be warned that you'll need exact change in US dollars. If you present them with a $20 bill for a $15 overstay, it's very likely that you won't be given change.

The **Cambodia government immigration site** (www. immigration.gov.kh/index.php?option=com_content&view=artic le&id=88&Itemid=77&lang=en) says that overstayers are also liable to pay the cost of an extended visa, but in practice overstayers are only charged the $5- or $6-per-day fee.

International movers

Find the right international movers or relocation specialists to help with your move to Cambodia.

Unless you are a diplomat or NGO employee, your personal effects shipped via mail or freight will be subject to duty (sometimes to a ridiculous degree). Because of this, many expats choose to move to Cambodia with nothing more than a couple of suitcases and start from scratch. But if you're attached to your stuff, here are some movers who can help you import your personal possessions to Cambodia.

PLANNING

Asian Tigers is known through the region for their good service. They offer moving and storage as well as relocation and home-search services.

Asian Tigers
86 Street 160, Phnom Penh
Tel : 023 880 951
www.asiantigersgroup.com

Cambodia Asian Tigers
www.asiantigersgroup.com/location.html?office=ca

If you only want the finest (or someone else is paying for your move), go with Crown Relocations. This global relocation specialist offers the full package, from moving to relocation services, including house-hunting, school-finding, and culture lessons. Crown is the company that huge multinational firms use to transfer their employees—they're pricey, but they're good.

Crown Relocations
115-116 Street 335, Toul Kork, Phnom Penh
Tel: 023 881 004
Email: phnompenh@crownrelo.com
www.crownrelo.com/cambodia

JVK Naga Movers is an international moving company that has offices all over Asia, including in Cambodia. Less expensive than the full-service movers, they are known for being able to deal adeptly with Cambodian bureaucracy.

JVK Naga Movers
27 Street 134, Phnom Penh
Tel: 023 724 746
Email: cambodia@jvkasia.com

Narita Logistics and Services executes moves in and out of the country as well as local moves. For international moves they work with FIDI Global Alliance, which has agents in more than 140 countries.

Narita Logistics and Services
21 Street 200, Phnom Penh
Tel: 023 210 013
phnom-penh.biz/cambodia-guide/phnom-penh/Service/
    narita-logistics-and-services

Those on a budget have reported success with Intra Co., which offers more of a DIY service than the relocation companies but is also much, much cheaper.

Intra Co.
2-3 Street 118, Phnom Penh
Tel: 023 428 596; 023 427 153; 023 217 095
www.intracambodia.com

Vaccinations

Some vaccinations you need to get before you come to Cambodia, and others you can get after you arrive.

It's best to make sure that you are up to date on all of your regular vaccinations before coming to Cambodia. Polio, diphtheria, and tetanus are the standards. It doesn't hurt to get a flu shot as well.

You can get a complete course of vaccinations in Phnom Penh for around $150, about 25 percent of what the same vaccinations would cost in London or New York. If your regular vaccinations are going to come due in the next few months, you can save quite a bit of money by waiting until you are in Cambodia to get them.

Other vaccinations that you should consider for Cambodia include the following:

Hepatitis A. This virus is spread through contaminated water and food, which Cambodia has in abundance. The vaccine requires a booster at 6 to 12 months, but you can get that in Cambodia if you haven't finished the course before you leave your home country.

Hepatitis B. Although part of the Kingdom's national immunization program, hepatitis B is nevertheless very common in Cambodia. HBV vaccine is therefore a must before coming, especially for kids or if you plan to have any medical procedures, tattoos, or unprotected sex with the locals. It requires three injections over a 6-month period, at 0, 1, and 6 months. A vaccine preparation combined with hepatitis A is available.

Typhoid. Also spread through contaminated food and water, typhoid is common in Cambodia, particularly in rural areas. Though a serious illness, it is treatable. Nevertheless, vaccination is strongly recommended before your trip to Cambodia or once you arrive if you intend to spend much time there or visit rural areas.

Japanese encephalitis. Caused by a mosquito-borne virus with animal vectors and most commonly spread near pigs, this is the disease whose vaccine seems to be the most favored choice of those who like to get a lot of vaccinations. There is no treatment for Japanese encephalitis, but the prevalence of Japanese encephalitis is low in Cambodia. Cases do occur on a regular basis, though, and the vaccine is recommended for those who will be spending extended periods of time in rural farming areas.

Rabies. Spread by bites from rabid animals, rabies is always fatal if untreated. It's most often recommended for those who are going to be far from medical care—if you plan to be anywhere where you will be more than 24 hours from a decent hospital, you should consider getting a rabies shot. Even if you get the vaccination, you'll still need to seek medical care, so many cost-sensitive travelers choose to skip the vaccination and take their chances.

Anti-malaria medication. You do not need to take anti-malarial medications in Cambodian cities. However, if you are traveling near forested areas, it's best to take them as a precaution. Doxycycline or Malarone are the recommended drugs of choice, and they can be purchased at U-Care Pharmacy in Phnom Penh or Siem Reap or at Pharmacie De La Gare on Monivong Boulevard in Phnom Penh. With or without it, always practice good mosquito protection.

Where to get vaccinated in Cambodia

For vaccinations in Phnom Penh, the Pasteur Institute is known to be one of the least expensive and most reliable choices in town, and expats swear by Dr. Scott at the Travellers Medical Clinic for everything tropical-disease-related. In Siem Reap, the Naga Clinic also offers vaccinations.

Pasteur Institute
BP 983-5 Monivong Boulevard, Phnom Penh
Tel: 023 426 009
www.pasteur-kh.org

Travellers Medical Clinic
88 Street 108, Phnom Penh
Tel: 023 306 802
www.travellersmedicalclinic.com

Naga Healthcare International Medical Center
660 Hup Guan Street (behind Central Market), Siem Reap
Tel: 092 793 180
www.nagahealthcare.com

For more information on what vaccinations are needed in Cambodia, please see the **United States CDC**'s page (wwwnc.cdc.gov/travel/destinations/cambodia.htm) and the UK government's NHS site, **Fit For Travel** (www.fitfortravel.nhs.uk/destinations/asia-(east)/cambodia.aspx).

Cost of living

No matter what your budget, Cambodia has something to offer — often for significantly less than what you pay at home.

One of the big attractions of Cambodia for visitors and long-term expats alike is the low cost of living here. If you're eating Cambodian food and living in a Khmer-style apartment deep in the provinces, it's possible to survive on less than $500 a month!

Most expats prefer to live in a city and enjoy a slightly more luxurious lifestyle, but even that is attainable for a few hundred dollars a month more. In a town where an iced coffee with condensed milk (trust us, it is delicious) goes for $0.50 and a six-pack of beer can be had for under $3, even a small paycheck goes a long way.

Here is a list of the costs of some basic items in Cambodia, including food and groceries, eating out, housing, utilities, transportation, and health care.

Costs of basic items in Cambodia

Prices given are for Phnom Penh in 2012. Prices outside of the city vary, but are generally lower (and when it comes to rent, much, much lower).

Food and groceries

1 liter (2 pints) fresh milk: $2
12 eggs: $1

1 baguette: $1-2
1 kg (2.2 lbs) apples: $2.80
1 kg (2.2 lbs) cucumbers: $0.80
1 kg (2.2 lbs) beef: $8-9
1 bottle red wine: $7-15
1 can beer: $0.40-0.60
1 bottle spirits (Absolut, Jameson, Bacardi): $8-12

Dining out

Iced coffee with sweet milk: $0.50
Cambodian pork and rice: $1
Medium-sized Blizzard at Dairy Queen: $2.50
Pizza: $5-15
Beer: $0.75-2
Mixed drink: $2-3
Dinner at an upscale restaurant: $12-20
Dinner at a mid-range Western restaurant: $6-8
Dinner at a Cambodian restaurant: $3-5

Housing

1 night in a guesthouse: $6-30
1 room in a shared flat with other expats: $70-250/
    month
1-bedroom Khmer-style apartment: $170-220/month
2-bedroom Khmer-style apartment: $250-300/month
1-bedroom Western-style apartment: $300-500/month
2-bedroom Western-style apartment: $500-1000/month
House cleaner: $4-5 per day

Utilities

Water: $0.13/cubic meter (actual), $5 per month (usual)
Electricity: $0.18-0.30/kWh

Garbage: $1-10/month
Cable television: $5-15/month
Internet: $20-90/month (prices vary based on package)

Transportation

Tuk tuk ride across town: $2
Moto taxi ride: $0.50-$1.25
Car taxi from airport: $9
Tuk tuk from airport: $4-7
1 liter gas: $1.35
Moto: $500-2,000

Health care

Appointment with a Western doctor: $40-85
Appointment with a local doctor: $5-50
Eye doctor appointment: $10
Basic lab tests: $30-85

Other

Gym membership: $30-150
Khmer lesson: $5 for one person, $6 for two people
Movie ticket in Phnom Penh: $3

Budgeting for your move

Many would-be expats with their eye on Cambodia wonder how much they need to save before they take the plunge. The answer is: not much.

As with any international move, before you relocate to Cambodia it's best to have three months' budget saved in advance (six, really, if you're a responsible type). How much that budget is depends on where and how you're planning to live in Cambodia.

Rent. Be prepared to pay one month's rent plus one or two months' deposit in advance. Plan to spend $170 to $300 per month on rent in Phnom Penh, less if you'll be in a rural area.

Job-hunting. If you're planning to work, figure on spending at least a month job-hunting. Yes, teaching jobs can be easy to find (with lots of caveats), but the good ones aren't. It's best not to get yourself stuck in a situation where you're forced to take the first job that comes along, because in Cambodia there are a lot of teaching gigs that are really unpleasant.

Additional expenses. If you'll be living in a city, plan on spending another $200 a week on food, transportation, and entertainment. If you're willing to live quite frugally (and you aren't planning on getting sauced every night), you can live on $600 or $700 a month in Phnom Penh, but it won't be nearly as much fun. If you're volunteering in the provinces, you can easily live on $500 a month or less, mainly because you won't have the opportunity to eat at expat restaurants, drink at expat bars, or do any of the other things that expats like to do in the major cities.

Summing up. If you're going to be in the provinces, budget at least a $2,000 nest egg to get started. If you'll be living in the city, plan for $3,000. However, the more you save to put into your nest egg, the easier life will be for you once you get here. Although many expats arrive in Cambodia with nothing, after spending some time here you'll soon realize that you don't want to be one of them.

Lazy beach

Relaxing on Koh Rong Samloem

Retro design

Hand-painted signs dot Phnom Penh's streets.

Part three

Living in Cambodia

Once you make the move to Cambodia, you'll have a lot to do — and we're here to help!

First you have to decide where to live: most expats choose Phnom Penh, Siem Reap, or Sihanoukville. We've got advice on homes and apartments, from long-term guesthouses to stay in while you look for an apartment to advice on buying property and hiring household staff and information about utilities.

We've got practical advice about how currency works in Cambodia (it's more complicated than it might seem), tips on how to get a local SIM card and open a bank account, and the information you need to know about sending and receiving mail.

Once you're ready to get around town, head to the Transportation section to learn how to take a tuk tuk or moto taxi or even get your own driver's license. We cover road safety, how to deal with police, and other transportation options, including Cambodia's long-distance buses and international flights.

It's also important for expats to stay healthy in Cambodia. Find out the recommended hospitals, doctors, and clinics, plus the pharmacies where you'll get real international medications. We also cover common ailments, dental issues, and eye care. Make sure to get a decent health insurance policy, but you may be one of those for whom travel insurance will do the trick. Since many expats also choose to seek medical care abroad, we've got recommendations for the easiest medical getaways.

Be sure to stay safe. In the Safety and security section we cover robberies, bag-snatchings, and hotel and apartment break-ins, and give you some emergency numbers and tips for dealing with the police, just in case. Oh, and some reasons why you shouldn't do illegal drugs in Cambodia.

Specifically for women, we have advice about what to wear and how to stay safe; in addition, the Health and medical care section covers women's health issues. We also have advice about your love life and your family life, with sections on sex and dating, gay culture in Cambodia, and raising kids in Cambodia, including some school recommendations.

Life in the Kingdom

Women in Battambang buy ingredients to make dinner.

Where to live in Cambodia

Whether you prefer Sihanoukville's beaches, Phnom Penh's city vibe, or Siem Reap's small-town feel, there are many places in Cambodia to settle down and call home.

Most expats have a pretty good idea of where they want to live in Cambodia before they move, because of where their new job is located or because they fell in love with a particular place on a previous visit. Phnom Penh and Siem Reap are the most popular cities for expats, but Sihanoukville has beaches, Battambang is charming, and Kep and Kampot are the definite up-and-comers in Cambodia. And then there are the provinces. . .

If you're planning on moving to Phnom Penh, we also have a handy neighborhood guide to help you decide where to live in the city.

Phnom Penh

Phnom Penh is Cambodia's capital city, home to between 2 and 3 million Cambodians and the great majority of the country's foreign expatriates. Some regard Phnom Penh as a charmless agglomeration of crumbling colonial buildings and towering architectural monstrosities, but to the expats who call it home it's a vibrant city steeped in history and full of excitement.

Because it's a big, busy metropolis, Phnom Penh offers an easy life for expats unwilling to give up the conveniences of home. Dozens of coffee shops have popped up in recent months, there are better grocery stores than you'll find in many other Southeast Asian cities, and there are even two brand new big-screen, air-conditioned movie theaters showing Hollywood blockbusters.

The infrastructure in Phnom Penh is also quite good. The water is pretty much drinkable (although no one risks it), power cuts are rare compared to places like Sihanoukville, and high-speed internet is available.

Perhaps most enticing are the many job opportunities in Phnom Penh, due to the presence of several hundred NGOs (non-governmental organizations) and even more

INTERVIEW WITH AN EXPAT

Why did you decide to live in Phnom Penh?

I moved to Phnom Penh to be closer to the Push Pull Cambodia weaving center and our sewing partners. I originally settled in Siem Reap and was hesitant to leave, but Phnom Penh is much closer to the hub of our business activities.

What is the best thing about living in Phnom Penh?

I've come to appreciate the energy of Phnom Penh. There's certainly more bustle here — more art happenings, more concerts, more events generally. I also love that there are restaurants that serve gluten-free pasta and desserts in Phnom Penh!

What is the worst thing about living in Phnom Penh?

The transient nature of Cambodia is difficult, regardless of your city of residence. One thing I noticed more in Phnom Penh is how difficult it is to walk from place to place. Nothing is terribly far, but sidewalks are often extensions of homes and shops and not passable. I'd love to be able to walk down the street without actually having to step into the street and the traffic.

Leigh Morlock
co-founder, Push Pull Cambodia
pushpullcambodia.com

English schools. Salaries are also higher in Phnom Penh than elsewhere in the country.

In addition, the city is home to dozens of expat-oriented bars and pubs, including many, many girly bars, a couple of nightclubs, and even a rock-n-roll bar. Phnom Penh is the only city in Cambodia with any real nightlife to speak of, so if this is important to you, you'll either have to move here or do a lot of weekend commuting.

Where to live in Phnom Penh

BKK1. BKK1 is the center of the Phnom Penh expat scene, where you will find the most expensive luxury apartments, posh coffee shops, and stores aimed at foreigners. Many NGOs are based here, and the real-estate prices reflect this fact. Expats often choose to live in BKK1 because they feel safer living among other foreigners, although in reality there can be more crimes against expats here than elsewhere in the city. That said, there is no denying that the amenities in BKK1 are fantastic, from spas to boutique shopping to high-end restaurants.

Riverside. Cheaper than BKK1, Phnom Penh's Riverside location is packed with Western restaurants, bars, and tourists. Because of the many girly bars in the area and the annoyance of persistent tuk tuk drivers and children selling books, many expats write off the Riverside as a place to live, which is a shame. Expats who do live in the area appreciate the proximity to the Tonle Sap — it's a great place to exercise. The neighborhood also features two all-day markets, Psar Cha and Psar Kandal, and a wealth of restaurants and bars at all price levels.

LIVING

Toul Sleng. Toul Sleng is the next big thing in terms of expat neighborhoods: it's popular with those in the under-40 crowd who are slightly more bohemian or have been priced out of BKK1. Prices in Toul Sleng are much lower than elsewhere in the city, but residents complain of constant power outages that more affluent areas seem to avoid.

Russian Market. To the south of Toul Sleng is Russian Market, which is fairly far from the city center but has a number of things to recommend it, including many coffee shops and excellent restaurants and inexpensive single-family-home and villa rentals.

Toul Kork. For those looking for luxurious detached house rentals or dirt-cheap apartments, Toul Kork has it all, but at the price of being a good 25-plus minutes outside of the city center, near the Phnom Penh airport. Many Korean expats favor the area, so the neighborhood has an abundance of Korean restaurants. Because Toul Kork is on the outskirts, owning some sort of transportation is essential for those who live there.

Siem Reap

The other major choice for expats is Siem Reap. Siem Reap means "Siam defeated" and refers to a 16th-century Khmer victory over what is now Thailand. The city is a major tourist destination due to its proximity to the temples of Angkor, and as a result it has lots in the way of infrastructure, modern hotels, and restaurants. That also means higher prices at Western restaurants and for transportation—that is, until you learn to bargain in Khmer.

Siem Reap is warmer than Phnom Penh and has a longer wet season. The countryside around the town is gorgeous,

INTERVIEW WITH AN EXPAT

Why did you decide to live in Siem Reap?

Amazing people, great weather, vast range of food, cheap everything, business opportunities, Angkor Wat on my doorstep, and my girlfriend, who is Cambodian.

What is the best thing about living in Siem Reap?

The relaxed way of life and the beautiful people, who inspire me daily.

What is the worst thing about living in Siem Reap?

The corruption in every place you look — the rich getting absurdly richer and the poor getting obscenely poorer.

Daniel Venn
owner, Lemongrass Garden Spa
www.lemongrassgarden.com,
Siem Reap

filled with rice paddies and ancient temples. The Western expat scene, although not huge, is vibrant, with many artists and photographers making their home here. Thanks to a large population of Korean and Japanese expats, Siem Reap has many Korean and Japanese restaurants.

Although the city is sleepier than Phnom Penh, expats who live in Siem Reap swear that the loveliness of the town, and the fact that the locals speak more English because of the tourism industry, more than make up for the lack of nightlife. Siem Reap has a thriving culinary scene, and some of the best restaurants in Cambodia are located here. You can find foreign food of all different stripes and even a handful of cooking schools. There's also a lot going on in Siem Reap's arts community, involving both local and foreign expat artists, and a number of up-and-coming galleries.

Cambodian skyscrapers

Phnom Penh's Riverside has apartments of all shapes and sizes.

Angkorian sunrise

Proximity to the temples of Angkor are a bonus for Siem Reap expats.

Seaside resort

Sunset in Kep

Beach town

Sihanoukville's Serendipity beach

Cambodian modern

Architectural styles from New Khmer to French Colonial can be found around Phnom Penh.

Indochina past

Battambang is known for its lovely French Colonial buildings.

Provincial living

The Cambodian provinces offer a slower way of life.

Mini Angkor

Battambang is also known for its ancient temples.

Battambang

Battambang is technically the second-largest city in Cambodia, but it feels like a laid-back, sleepy burg. Filled with lovely colonial buildings and surrounded by Angkorian temples, Battambang has a unique small-town appeal that hasn't seemed to have caught on with tourists yet. That said, the infrastructure is lacking, there's no nightlife, and don't count on being able to buy your favorite foreign food products in a town this small.

One of the last holdouts of the Khmer Rouge, the city is now home to a population of a quarter million, but it feels much, much smaller. Battambang doesn't have a lot of expats, but there's a fair-sized French population in town. Retirees and Phnom Penh expats looking for a place to dry out or a quieter existence love the place.

Ownership of the town has passed between the French, the Thais, and Cambodia for hundreds of years, and the influence of all three is significant. In addition to the French colonial buildings, you'll find a number of French and French-influenced restaurants in town, as well as excellent Thai food—the city is a major trading partner with Thailand. There are also several cooking schools in town offering lessons in Khmer and Thai cuisine.

Sihanoukville

Sihanoukville is Cambodia's top beach destination and a favorite with those looking for a beachside vibe. It's also got a bit of a reputation as a party city, for better or worse. Some expats say that the seedy reputation is undeserved, while others seem to delight in it.

Many child-protection NGOs are based in Sihanoukville, but English-teaching jobs in town generally pay less than in

INTERVIEW WITH AN EXPAT

Why did you decide to live in Sihanoukville?

I came to Sihanoukville for vacation, fell in love, and saw lots of opportunity for business. I felt it was a good place to try to start my own first business. Since everything is so cheap, the risk isn't such a great one.

What is the best thing about living in Sihanoukville?

I love the chilled-out lifestyle in Sihanoukville and being near the beach.

What is the worst thing about living in Sihanoukville?

As a business owner, the hardest thing is finding staff and the work ethic of people in general. Otherwise, the sense of being helpless when it comes to legal issues.

Christophe Hanson
owner, Le Mac Restaurant,
Sihanoukville

LIVING

Phnom Penh. There are lots of expats in Sihanoukville; most of them seem to be middle-aged men. Many from the Pattaya party scene migrated here when Thailand began cracking down on expat visas. The city is also popular with Russian expats, who own many of the businesses in the Victory Hill area of town.

The newest of Cambodia's major cities, Sihanoukville was founded in the 1950s. Now the place is filled with construction sites and new luxury hotels looking to capitalize on the tourism boom. During the high season the town and its beaches teem with young backpackers looking to eat "happy" pizzas and sleep in each other's dorm beds. The town's nightlife is active, if not very sophisticated, but it calms down and can get pretty quiet during the low season.

There's no decent medical care in town, and a narrower range of shopping, so expats find themselves making frequent trips to Phnom Penh to see a doctor or to stock up on the essentials. For all the downsides, many of the beaches around Sihanoukville are beautiful, and the islands offshore are positively stunning.

Kep and Kampot

Quiet Kampot and Kep are slowly gaining traction with foreign expats, because of their beautiful scenery, available land, and gradually improving infrastructure. There aren't a lot of job opportunities here, although a number of Christian NGOs call Kampot home. For those who find Phnom Penh too loud and busy, Kep and Kampot each offer a simpler, more relaxed lifestyle.

Kep was once Cambodia's top seaside resort, but much of it was destroyed during the Khmer Rouge period. You can still see burned-out mansions dotting the town. Kep is only

INTERVIEW WITH AN EXPAT

Why did you decide to live in Kampot?

We moved to **Kampot** from Sihanoukville in 2008, when things there started to get a little more developed. It allowed us to live in the countryside, as well as being quite close to a town.

What is the best thing about living in Kampot?

The natural beauty of the town and surrounding country.

What is the worst thing about living in Kampot?

In terms of restaurants catering to expat tastes, Sihanoukville has more choices.

Simon Oliver
blogger
www.talesfromanexpat.com

now becoming a popular tourist attraction, and most of the expats who live here are running guesthouses or otherwise working in the tourism industry. Kep is known for having the best seafood in the country.

Kampot is just a few kilometers from the Gulf of Thailand, but it's still a sleepy riverside town; many of the hotels and guesthouses are situated on the Kampot River. It's an up-and-coming tourist destination, and expats are also quickly discovering its charms. Its small-town feel and cheap housing make the town ripe for an influx of foreigners.

The Cambodian provinces

Of course these six cities do not Cambodia make, and there are expats living all over the country. Prices in the countryside are very, very cheap and you can rent a house for next to nothing. Plus, immersion is one of the fastest ways to learn the language, and the further you get from the big city the more amenable locals are to helping you practice your Khmer.

If living in the provinces is a great way to learn Khmer, be warned that it's a difficult life at first if you are on your own and without Khmer language skills. That said, many people have settled down in the countryside with their Khmer partners and enjoy the peace and quiet that can be found there (if you don't mind the roosters and the karaoke).

Smaller cities, especially along the borders, usually have at least a few expat residents. Koh Kong, for example, has many Western-owned businesses and at least a couple Peace Corps volunteers at any given time. The same is true for Ratanakiri and most of the other small cities in the country. Even Poipet—believed by many to be the cesspool of Cambodia—has a handful of expats who call the place home.

LIVING

INTERVIEW WITH AN EXPAT

Why did you decide to live in Ratanakiri?

During the early part of graduate studies I decided to conduct my research in the Central Highlands of Vietnam. Later I decided, for many reasons, that Cambodia suited me better. As I had already been looking into the issues concerning highland peoples in that part of Indochina, research in Ratanakiri, just across the border from the Vietnamese Central Highlands, made sense.

What is the best thing about living in Ratanakiri?

The people. I have found the people in Ratanakiri to be very friendly. The weather also. It gets much cooler up there than in lowland Cambodia.

What is the worst thing about living in Ratanakiri?

It's a very small town. While I like knowing lots of the people who live there, and they knowing me, like all small towns it can be very gossipy. And there's also a smaller selection of good places to eat.

Jared Cahners
anthropologist in training

Homes and apartments

Depending on how long you intend to stay in Cambodia, you may choose to stay in a long-term guesthouse, find an apartment or house, or buy property and build your own.

Most new expats end up moving at least a few times before they find the perfect place, so it's usually better to start out in a guesthouse or a short-term lease when you first arrive. This will allow you to get the lay of the land, as it were, and decide not only where you want to live but what housing attributes are most important to you. For example, is having hot water a priority? An oven in your kitchen? A security guard? Are you willing to walk up more than one flight of stairs? All vital questions you should know the answers to before you settle into a permanent home — and your answers may change after your first few months in the country!

We've got recommendations for where to stay while you're looking for something more permanent, how to find long-term hotels and guesthouses, how to locate shared apartments, and, once you're ready to take the plunge, tips on how to find your own apartment. We've even got information on buying property in Cambodia, if you're so inclined.

And once you're settled, you'll want to know about utilities, including garbage collection, electricity and water, and internet and cable television. We've also got some tips for hiring and managing household staff.

LIVING

69

Long-term hotels and guesthouses

If you're here for a few weeks up to a few months, guesthouses offer an easy solution for those not ready to put down roots quite yet, with the added bonus of fresh sheets and towels without having to lift a finger.

Most guesthouses in town are willing to negotiate rates for long-term stays. On the low end of the scale, backpacker venues such as Okay Guesthouse in Phnom Penh will rent their $7 rooms for $5 per night for long-term guests.

Mid-range places like Aqua Boutique Guesthouse on Street 63 in Phnom Penh offer deals on rooms for guests staying more than one week, from $25 and up. For those looking for something a little more swanky, a two-bedroom apartment with kitchen and dining area goes for more than $200 per night at the Himawari Hotel Apartments.

In Siem Reap, some of the better budget guesthouses and hostels are Siem Reap Rooms, Golden Temple Villa near the Old Market, Golden Mango Inn, HI Siem Reap, and the Rosy Guesthouse.

In Battambang, Chhaya Serviced Apartments offer serviced apartments with kitchenettes for $270 per month. Banon Hotel is another good mid-range hotel choice, and Royal Hotel is a good option for the budget set, with rooms starting at $3 per night.

Finding a shared apartment

If you're not quite ready to sign a lease or don't want to live alone, a shared apartment is the way to go. It's quite easy to find already established shared apartments to join, or to set up a new one on your own (although that will necessitate getting a lease).

Apartment shares in Phnom Penh run from $70 to $250 for a bedroom in a shared flat. The cheaper ones are usually located outside the center of town in Khmer-style apartments, where residents may have to forego such Western conveniences as ovens and kitchen counter space. The more expensive ones are in BKK1 and offer all of the amenities, often including swimming pools and gyms. In Siem Reap the prices are lower, and in smaller cities even less than that.

In a shared apartment situation, generally either long- or short-term stays are acceptable. One housemate is usually the leaseholder, and all housemates split the shared bills, such as utilities and internet. Because of the high cost of electricity and Cambodia's heat, it's good to discuss how the electricity bills will be split—if one housemate works at home or likes to use a lot of air-conditioning, it can make bills substantially higher. Most houseshare situations also hire a cleaner two or three times a week, the cost of which is also shared.

To find apartment shares in Phnom Penh, check out Expat Advisory and The Cambodia Parent's Network. To find apartment shares in Siem Reap, try the Siem Reap Expats Facebook Group. To find apartment shares in Kampot and

Living large

Whether you rent an apartment or stay in a hotel, Cambodia has lots of options.

LIVING

Kep, visit the Kampot and Kep Noticeboard on Facebook.
To find apartment shares in Sihanoukville, check out the
Sihanoukville Expats Facebook group or the Sihanoukville
Online Forums. (See the **Web resources** section (page 177)
for more information.)

Finding your own apartment

Renting an apartment is usually the most economical way to
stay for a while in most cities in Cambodia. Most apartments
come fully furnished and landlords are willing to sign leases
of just three months (and sometimes less than that), so the
savings over a guesthouse can be substantial.

There are two ways to find apartments in Cambodia, the
cheap way and the expensive way. Perhaps unsurprisingly,
the least expensive path involves a fair amount of legwork
but can result in some outstanding deals.

Using an agent is usually a pricier way to find an
apartment, but if you're looking for something high end,
this is how to proceed. For those on a budget, using an
agent usually adds about $50 per month to your rent—the
landlords raise the rent to cover the cost of the agent's fee,
and they tend to charge those who use agents more anyway.

However, an agent can help with the lease and act as
an intermediary between you and the landlord. Be advised,
though, that agents will usually side with the landlords
(that's who's paying them, after all), and most people who've
worked with rental agents in Cambodia would probably
agree that they leave a lot to be desired, since as a group
they tend to have a highly flexible approach to the concept
of "truth." However, if you tell an agent what you are looking
for you'll almost certainly be shown a number of properties
and be able to sign a lease and possibly even move in the
same day.

In Phnom Penh, two recommended agents are:

Art the Homefinder
Tel: 012 422 126
artthehomefinder.wordpress.com

Socheat Yim at KC Group Realty
Tel: 012 283 079; 099 234 506

In Siem Reap three recommended agents are:

Bruno L'Hoste at Siem Reap Properties
Tel: 012 808 916
www.siemreap-properties.info

Sophy
Tel: 012 376 448

Chanrith Wee
Tel: 012 224 228

If you want to find a better deal, your best bet is to search for apartments on your own. Decide what neighborhood you want to live in and walk around looking for "For Rent" signs. Calling the phone numbers on these signs can have mixed results. Often the landlords who don't speak English are willing to offer lower rates than the ones who do, so it's worth persevering or having a Khmer friend help you with the calls.

An easier way is to ask a trusted moto or tuk tuk driver to help you search for signs and assist with the negotiations. Your guesthouse may be able to recommend a driver for you, if you don't have a relationship with any drivers yet, but make sure they aren't trying to negotiate an agent's fee for themselves with the landlord. If they do find you an apartment, however, be sure to reward them generously.

LIVING

Buying property in Cambodia

Expats who want to buy property in Cambodia need to be prepared to grease a lot of palms. Technically, foreigners cannot own land in Cambodia. There are exceptions, however. Foreigners can own apartments in buildings as long as the apartments are not on the ground floor. They can also lease land and buildings (99-year renewable leases are popular in Cambodia). Some long-term expats buy property and put it in the name of a trusted Cambodian friend or spouse. And finally, land can be bought through a local company in which a foreigner has a minority share.

The process of buying property through a local company is relatively simple. You start a company where you are the 49 percent owner. The other 51 percent needs to be owned by a local (that is, Cambodian) partner. To safeguard their investment, wise expats require the local partner to sign a document (signature and thumbprint) stating that you have complete control over any land or property owned by the company and, furthermore, that the local partner agrees that you can replace him or her with another Cambodian at any time at your discretion. This allows you to replace your partner if the need ever arises.

For extra safety, you can divide the 51 percent among a couple of locals who don't know each other and set up a mortgage on the land to ensure that the land cannot be transferred without your consent. It's important to note that as a company you will be required to file tax documents each year, but since the company will not have income, you will only have to pay a small monthly fee and an end-of-year fee. The process is simple, but complicated enough that buying property should probably be undertaken only by those who intend to stay for a while.

Whether you intend to stay or not, be aware that Cambodia is notorious for land grabs, whereby the government sells off huge chunks of land to private companies, ignoring the fact that the land was already owned by someone else. Even foreigners have had their land taken in this manner. If you do intend to buy land, be sure to talk to at least a few professionals before you make the leap into ownership, and seriously consider the idea of long-term leasing first.

Utilities

Utilities are an endless source of headaches and amusement for expats in Cambodia. Wherever you live, garbage removal is sure to be frustrating, whether you're getting fleeced by the garbage company, cheated by your landlord, or forced to stand in a cloud of toxic fumes burning your garbage in a rice paddy somewhere. Water and electricity are a little better, in that the rates are published (but your landlord may charge you more). Internet and cable are the best of the bunch, and surprisingly good for a developing country.

Garbage

Knowing the cost of utilities is an important part of finding an apartment or house in Cambodia, and not knowing is one of the common ways that expats get ripped off.

In Phnom Penh and Sihanoukville, Canadian company **CINTRI** (www.cintri.com.kh) has a monopoly on garbage collection. In Phnom Penh the CINTRI bill is added to your electricity bill, which means that you can't get away with not paying it unless you want to live in the dark. The cost per month for a residential property that is a shophouse or single-family apartment is usually $1, but sometimes if the bill is in a foreigner's name the cost is bumped up to $10 per month. This is per building, though, so if a landlord with three apartments asks for $5 per month per apartment, remember that the landlord is only paying $1 per month for the whole building. Prices go up for villas, which cost $5, $10, or $20 a month depending on size. If you politely refuse, landlords will usually not charge for garbage. Businesses always pay more, usually around $10 per month but often much higher.

Prices for garbage collection in Sihanoukville are significantly higher, ranging from $10 per month to $50 per pickup, depending on location, whether the customer is business versus residential, and the whims of the CINTRI staff.

CINTRI has a poor reputation among expats. It has been known to raise the rates whenever dealing with foreigners and expat-owned businesses and to engage in behavior that many would consider extortionate, often backdating rate increases by several months. If possible, register your bill in a Khmer's name and have a Khmer go to the office for you to argue your case when CINTRI inevitably overcharges you. One thing to remember is that the prices are flexible. If they try to charge your business $50 a month, it's often possible to negotiate the fee down to $20 per month.

Outside of the big cities, most locals recycle plastics and cans and burn the rest.

Electricity and water

The cost of electricity in Cambodia is one of the highest in the world, and only about 15 percent of the country has access to it. The limited electricity that Cambodia generates is usually sold to its neighbors rather than designated for domestic use. In the cities prices are not too bad, but in the provinces they are outrageously high.

Moreover, outside of Phnom Penh and Siem Reap the electricity is very unreliable, particularly in Sihanoukville, where business owners must purchase generators to deal with the hours-long power cuts that always seem to happen in high season. In much of the countryside the only electricity comes from these generators or the alternative that many families use, car batteries. In the cities, though, power is provided by **EDC** (www.edc.com.kh).

Electricity is where landlords make a killing on tenants. The actual rates for electricity in Phnom Penh are 610 riel per kWh if you use under 50 kilowatts in a month, or 720 per kWh if you use over 100 kilowatts. Landlords, however, will try to charge you an average of 1,000 riel per kilowatt, which can end up costing you an additional $20 to $30 a month, all of which the landlord will pocket. If you are renting, negotiate this ahead of time and do not agree to pay more than the actual rate.

Businesses in Phnom Penh report paying higher rates, with prices varying depending on the business location and factors known only to EDC.

In Siem Reap, the reported rate is 820 riel per kWh. In Battambang it's 1,000 per kWh and in Kampot it's 1,000 per kWh. Businesses pay an additional surcharge. In Sihanoukville, the residential charge is 820 riel per kWh and up to 1,355 for businesses. In the provinces, the electricity can cost much more, 2,000 to 2,500 per kWh, if it's available at all.

Most Cambodians use charcoal, firewood, or gas to cook their dinners with. There is no municipal gas supply in Cambodia, but you can get a refill of a 15 kg portable gas tank for around $20. Have them weigh it at the store, as they will often try to sell half-full tanks for full price.

Although landlords will try and charge you $5 per month for water, the actual rates are much lower. In Phnom Penh, if you use less than 7 cubic meters of water per month the cost is 550 riel per cubic meter; up to 15 cubic meters per month, the cost is 770 riel per cubic meter. There's an additional 10 percent sewerage fee. The cost for one or two people per month usually averages around $0.50 to $1. If your landlord asks for $5 per month, ask to pay what's listed on the meter, or settle for $1 per month.

In Siem Reap, if you use less than 7 cubic meters per month, the cost is 1,100 riel per cubic meter; up to 15 cubic meters per month, the cost is 1,500 riel per cubic meter. There's an additional 10 percent sewerage fee. The cost per month for one or two people should be $1 or $2.

In Sihanoukville, if you use less than 7 cubic meters per month, the cost is 1,500 riel per cubic meter; up to 15 cubic meters per month, the cost is 1,800 riel per cubic meter. There's an additional 10 percent sewerage fee as well.

In all areas, the cost for water for businesses is higher.

And despite what you may have heard, the municipal water in Cambodia is completely safe to drink. However, because the pipes that bring it to you may be disgusting, it's worth having your home's water tested when you move in (you can take a sample to the Pasteur Institute in Phnom Penh) or install a filter. Bottled water is available in 20 L bottles. They cost $5 the first time you get one and $1 for each refill.

Internet and cable

There are a few companies providing cable television in Cambodia. **Phnom Penh Cable TV** (www.ppctv.com.kh) offers service in Phnom Penh, Siem Reap, Kampot, and Sihanoukville. Installation costs $50 and the monthly fee is $10 and includes connections to three televisions.

Cambodia Cable Television (www.cctv.com.kh) also offers cable service at the same price, but only in Phnom Penh. Both offer a range of channels in many languages, including many channels in English and many streamed from Hong Kong (including an array of American television programs) and Australia. Most landlords will not make you pay for cable if you ask not to.

In Sihanoukville there are more French and Russian channels, but also a good selection of English television. Check out Cam Kom Cable and Sihanoukville Cable. In Siem Reap, try Angkor Cable. Your landlord should be able to help you set it up. In Kampot, most go with Dara Cable, at a cost of $6 per month.

When it comes to internet access in Cambodia, you'll have many options. While most of them will not match the speeds you get at home, they're still pretty great for a developing country. Many expats choose to take advantage of the broad 3G coverage in the country by using a 3G modem. Popular packages are with phone providers such as **Metfone** (www.metfone.com.kh), who at time of writing are offering a monthly package of 4 GB for $12 and sell the portable modem for $30. Although the 3G modems are notoriously difficult, when the signal is good speeds can top 1 Mbps and they work in most busy parts of the country (including on long bus trips).

The most popular ISP in Cambodia is **Ezecom** (www. ezecom.com.kh), which offers coverage across most of the country. They have packages starting at $19, but if you're a serious user you won't be happy with the speeds on their cheaper plans. If you want to get more than 1 Mbps, expect to spend around $100 a month.

Hiring household staff

One of the great pleasures of living in Cambodia for many expats is never having to clean their house again. Hiring a cleaner, cook, nanny, driver, gardener, or security guard is a relatively easy task, and most expats and middle-class Cambodians have at least some household help. In fact, many houses in Cambodia are designed with a small bedroom meant to house a maid or cook (who can also double as a nanny).

Lest you think expats here are being self-indulgent, be aware that homes in Cambodia get incredibly dirty very quickly—Cambodia's dusty hot season, unpaved streets, and developing-industry grunginess make it difficult to keep your living space even minimally tidy. Many newly arrived expats vow that they will never hire someone to do their housework, but a few months of having to mop three times a week usually convinces them to give in and outsource their cleaning.

The cost of labor in Cambodia is shockingly low. A full-time household employee might receive less than $100 a month. If you're hiring a part-time cleaner, expect to pay between $4 and $5 per visit, so $40 a month for twice a week or $60 a month for three times a week. Many foreigners get away with paying far less (and locals certainly do), but once you calculate the cost of living in Cambodia, it's hard to justify paying staff wages that are borderline abusive.

Full-time employees work six or seven days a week, with occasional holidays. They will expect to receive a week off at Khmer New Year, when it is considered good form to give employees a cash gift equal to a week or two of their salary. Additionally, many employees will ask for an advance on their wages for Khmer New Year; it's important for Cambodians to go home bearing gifts for their families in the provinces during this time, especially if they are seen as wealthy—which they are if they work in the big city for a foreign employer.

Learning to live with Khmer staff can be a slow process, especially for those unused to having household help. Generally, staff are eager to learn, and although you may have to show your cook or cleaner what you want a few times, she will eventually figure it out. Be sure to give clear instructions. Expecting your staff to read your mind or even do the most logical thing is an exercise in futility and tends to result in a lot of headaches for all involved.

Most household help will not speak English but can be shown the basics. Many foreigners choose to also pay to send their household staff for English lessons, which is a simple way you can help make their life, and yours, significantly easier. There are also cooking classes in Khmer meant to teach staff how to cook Western dishes and follow Western hygiene standards for cooking. Additionally, Monument Books in Phnom Penh and Siem Reap stock a cookbook in Khmer meant for those cooking in foreign households. For nannies, there are also first-aid classes.

The best way to find household staff is through references from other expats, which you can locate on any of the expat forums listed in the **Web resources** section (page 177). As with any household staff, be aware that what you spend on dinner might be what your staff earns over several weeks (and they're supporting eight family members in the provinces). So don't put them in the way of temptation and try not to leave cash lying around the house. Usually this is not an issue, but it's better to be safe than sorry, and to avoid situations where your mislaying of some cash leads you to fire an employee who, it turns out, was perfectly innocent.

LIVING

What to do when you first arrive

Once you get to Cambodia, there are a few things you'll want to do right away.

As soon as you've found a place to stay, put your stuff away (but be sure to follow the precautions in the Safety and security section in order to keep your possessions safe). Then you'll want to get a phone and a Cambodian SIM card so you can start making and receiving local calls.

Next, get your documents together and set up a local bank account. Most of the ATMs in the country that accept international cards charge $4 or $5 per transaction, so the sooner you set up a local bank account, the better.

It's also worthwhile to get a post office box so you can receive mail. It doesn't cost much and it's more reliable than having the mail delivered to your home. We'll also explain how to send and receive mail in Cambodia.

How to get a phone and SIM card

Back in the day, getting a SIM card in Cambodia was no small task. You had to have a Cambodian sponsor or else you'd be stuck with an overpriced tourist SIM especially for foreigners. But those days are long gone, and now anyone can get a regular SIM card in Cambodia with relatively little hassle.

Cambodia has one of the most competitive mobile markets in the world, with nine phone carriers for a population of about 15 million. Although it's a complicated market, it's good news for consumers, who can take advantage of numerous special promotions and deals as the companies vie for new customers.

The Cambodian cell companies are: Cellcard/Mobitel, Metfone, Smart, Starcard, qb, Beeline, Mfone, Hello, and Excell.

Each brand has different levels of coverage around the country (although all seem to work well in Phnom Penh and Siem Reap) and different price packages. To complicate matters, making cross-network calls can be expensive and difficult, which is why you'll often see Cambodians with three or even four cellphones in hand.

Most expats, though, choose pre-paid Cellcard plans due to their English-speaking staff and cheap data packages. Smart is also a good bet for international long-distance calls — rates are currently 7 cents per minute and there are promotions for overseas calls for as low as 4 cents per minute — although it's not considered as reliable for day-to-day phoning.

You can buy SIM cards at any of the phone shops in Cambodia, but it's best to get them directly from the mobile company. Carriers are required to keep a copy of your passport on file, but many of the small shops don't bother with this requirement. If you lose your phone, though, you can easily get a replacement SIM if your passport has been registered. If not, you're out of luck. Additionally, phone shops charge a large markup on SIM cards; ones that will cost $2 at the carrier office will be $10 at a shop.

To purchase a SIM card, just bring a passport with a valid visa to the office. You'll be offered a variety of cards starting at around $2. More expensive cards don't actually have more value, just supposedly lucky combinations

LIVING

of digits in the phone number. At Cellcard, SIMs cost $2 and you're required to add at least $1 in credit when you purchase one to activate it. In-network calls cost 5 to 7 cents per minute and it's 8 cents per minute for cross-network calls. International calls cost 20 cents per minute, or 10 cents per minute if you dial 177 before the country code.

If you're looking for a data plan on your phone, Cellcard is also the carrier of choice. They offer a monthly package with 2 GB for $5. To activate, just text INET3 to 6767. You'll probably need to configure the following information:

APN: cellcard
Username: mobitel
Password: mobitel

Phones are available at any of the thousands of phone shops all over the country. The cheapest are Nokias, which sell for $20 to $22 and have a handy flashlight feature. Smartphones are also available all over the country, and most phone stores can unlock the phone you brought from home.

In Phnom Penh, Cambodian-American phone whiz Danny at City Phone is the man to visit with all of your phone repair issues and needs.

City Phone
33 Street 128 (Kampuchea Krom), Phnom Penh
Tel: 023 216 456; 013 733 777

Cellcard
33 Sihanouk Boulevard, Phnom Penh
Tel: 012 800 800

50 Sivutha Street, Siem Reap
Tel: 012 829 909; 017 829 909

98-100Eo Street 3½, Battambang
Tel: 092 507 777; 017 776 888

265Eo, Street Ekareach, Sihanoukville
Tel: 012 444 314; 012 988 985
Email: helpline@mobitel.com.kh
www.cellcard.com.kh

Smart Mobile
464A Monivong Boulevard, Phnom Penh
Tel: 010 201 000

50, Group 1, Mondul 2, Siem Reap
Tel: 010 201 262

612Eo, Prek MohaTep Village, Battambang
Tel: 010 201 264

137 Group 17 Mondul 1 Sangkat 2, Mitapheab
   City, Sihanoukville
Tel: 010 201 263
www.smart.com.kh/en

Banking

Many expats choose to keep their bank accounts from home open and use them as their primary source of cash, but with ATMs charging up to $5 per transaction for foreign cards in Cambodia (and the home banks often charging the same), it makes sense to open a bank account in Cambodia if you're going to be here for more than a couple of months.

ATM machines abound, although most charge a hefty $4 or $5 fee for international cards. The exception is Canadia Bank, which charges no fee on ATM transactions. You can find red Canadia ATMs at the airports.

All ATM machines that accept foreign ATM cards dispense US dollars. Most will not dispense riel unless you have a local bank account. Another thing to note is that the ATMs in Cambodia tend to dispense $100 and $50 bills, and most businesses can't make change for bills this large. So plan your purchases carefully and try to break large bills whenever you can—hotels, grocery stores, and tourist-oriented restaurants are good bets.

Setting up a bank account in Cambodia is relatively easy. Most banks require a passport with a valid long-stay visa and a copy of your lease or an employment letter.

ANZ Royal Bank (anzroyal.com) is one of the most popular choices for expats due to its relationship with Australia-based ANZ bank.

They have branches in Phnom Penh, Siem Reap, Poipet, Battambang, Kampong Cham, and Sihanoukville and 127 ATM locations across Cambodia.

To set up a bank account at ANZ Royal you must provide a valid long-stay visa and a signed letter from your employer verifying your employment in Cambodia. Technically a copy of your lease or residency information is also required, but it is not usually asked for. The minimum opening deposit is $500 for a Convenience Plus account and the monthly charge is $1 if you maintain a balance of $500, or $3 if you do not. They offer internet banking and international transfers at reasonable rates.

ACLEDA Bank (www.acledabank.com.kh) is one of Cambodia's largest banks, with more than 230 branches in the country—there's one nearly anywhere you'd want to go. They offer online bill payment to the utilities companies and some of the mobile phone carriers, as well as internet banking.

Opening a current account at ACLEDA requires a minimum opening deposit of $1,000 in US dollars or nine other currencies and an ongoing balance of $500 or more.

Canadia Bank (www.canadiabank.com.kh) is one of the largest local banks in Cambodia and another expat favorite. They offer fee-free withdrawals from their ATMs. They have nearly 40 branches with 50 ATMs across the country. Current accounts are available in Cambodian riel, US dollars, and Thai baht and require a $200 minimum deposit. Bring your passport with valid visa.

Mail

The mail system in Cambodia leaves a lot to be desired. Employees of the Cambodia Post make less than $50 a month, and you can tell. Expats estimate that only 80 to 90 percent of the mail they send gets to its destination. Incoming mail usually arrives—but often takes two to five months. Having a post office box seems to improve the odds.

Often small postcards and envelopes disappear en route, so having things sent in large manila envelopes is a good idea. International shippers also can't track packages once they arrive in Cambodia; it's not unheard of for a package to enter the country and then not get delivered for another 90 days. That's just Cambodia, and it's why many companies are unwilling to deliver to Cambodian addresses. However, things are getting better—Amazon.com will even ship some items to Cambodia these days.

LIVING

Receiving mail in Cambodia

There are a few things you can do to make sure your
mail arrives:

Don't expect the post office to deliver to private homes.
They will, but only if your house is really easy to find. Like,
really easy. Since many apartments are not easy to find, or
don't have addresses on them that make sense, or don't have
house numbers at all, it's often best to get a post office box.

**When the post office does deliver to your house, they
will usually try once and then give up.** And they will not
necessarily leave a note.

Prepare to tip. If post office personnel successfully deliver
mail to your home, they will expect a small tip for their
trouble, usually between 1,000 riel and $1. If you do not tip,
next time they may deliver your mail to the garbage can.

**Always have senders put your phone number on the
package.** Often the post office is more willing to call you than
to try to deliver, so having your number on the package is
usually the fastest way to get mail.

Check the book. If you are expecting a package, it's also
worth going to the post office and looking through their book
with the list of package arrivals. Sometimes they will not
want to show you, but insist politely and you'll usually find
a long list of packages that have not been delivered neatly
inscribed inside.

Fees. When you do pick up a package at the post office,
they will sometimes charge you a seemingly arbitrary
fee—usually only for packages that are sent registered,

but these packages do arrive more quickly and reliably. Sometimes they will ask you to open the package in front of them. If you are receiving anything of value, be aware that Cambodia has a very high import tax, in addition to a value-added tax, and you can be hit with huge fees on arrival. This is why most people do not advise shipping electronics and other expensive goods.

Missing in transit. Some expats have also reported that their mail has been opened and items have occasionally gone missing—another reason to abandon the idea of having valuables shipped to you. However, most expats with a post office box have a relatively easy time receiving their mail.

Sending mail in Cambodia

Sending mail in Cambodia can be a crapshoot. Cambodia Post isn't very reliable, and the costs can vary depending on the mood and relative wealth of the woman at the counter. Most of the foreign shippers in Cambodia are locally run franchises, so the service you have come to expect back home will probably not be forthcoming.

For incoming mail, UPS often requires you to use a broker to settle your customs tax, which can end up being very, very expensive. Most report good luck with DHL, but it does not come cheap.

EMS is Cambodia Post's package service, and the prices are generally much, much lower than those of the international services, and most report good results using them. EMS has nine offices in Phnom Penh and local offices in all of the other provinces. Mail companies like DHL are generally considered safe but expensive.

EMS: Cambodia Post
Head office: Street 13 and Street 102, Phnom Penh
119.15.82.82/www/?page_id=340

TNT Cambodia
28 Monivong Boulevard, Phnom Penh
Tel: 023 430 922
www.tnt.com/express/en_kh/site/home.html

Cambodia Post: Main Phnom Penh Branch
Street 13 and Street 102, Phnom Penh
Tel: 023 426 062; 023 725 370
www.cambodiapost.com.kh

Cambodia Post: Sihanoukville
Ekareach Street, near Victory Hill, Sihanoukville
Tel: 034 933 526

Cambodia Post: Kampot
Riverside Road, about 500 meters from the bridge, Kampot

Cambodia Post: Siem Reap
Pokambor Avenue, about 500 meters from the roundabout,
Siem Reap
Tel: 063 963 446; 063 760 000

Getting a post office box

Post office boxes are inexpensive and exponentially increase the chances that you will actually receive your mail. Some post offices have multiple box sizes, including boxes large enough for packages. If you get a smaller box, they will usually put a notice in your box stating that you have a package and you can pick it up from behind the counter. Sometimes they won't bother with the notice, so if you're expecting a package it's worth looking at their incoming packages notebook to see if your name is listed. Also, small envelopes get lost far more often than large ones, so if you're having a friend or family member post you something, consider asking them put it in a padded envelope. Additionally, be aware that if you leave a package at the post office for more than a week or two, or don't answer your phone when they call, the post office employees will consider your package abandoned and take it home.

Phnom Penh. In Phnom Penh, head to the main post office on Street 102 and Street 13, near the Riverside. The cost is 50,000 riel per year ($12.50). Some expats report being asked for a copy of their passport and visa, and others do not. Likewise, some are asked to pay a 2,000-riel "administrative fee" in order to get a post office box. Although all post office boxes must be registered at the main post office, there are actually two post offices with boxes; the other is on Sihanouk Boulevard across from Wat Moha Montrei. You can request either post office when you register your box.

Sihanoukville. In Sihanoukville, the price is considerably higher, at $30 a year. Register at the main post office on Ekareach Street near Victory Hill. Again, be prepared to show your passport and visa, although most people aren't asked to do so.

Kampot. In Kampot, the cost is $20 per year. Bring a copy of your visa and passport to the post office on the riverside, about 500 meters from the bridge, and you'll be assigned a box on the spot.

Siem Reap. In Siem Reap the cost is between $15 and $25 per year, but all of the boxes are usually full. It's worth trying every once in a while, though, because new ones do become available when people leave or let their registration lapse.

Transportation

There are many ways to get around town, but each has its own frustrations.

One of the first challenges newcomers to Cambodia have to deal with is transportation. We've got some simple tips for taking tuk tuks that will make your life a lot easier — and that apply to taking moto taxis as well.

To get out of town, most locals rely on long-distance buses, but there are also flights out of Siem Reap and Phnom Penh. Just be careful of the land crossings. They inevitably require patience, and usually bribes as well.

If you're ready to drive your own moto, you'll need to get a license and be prepared to deal with the local police on a regular basis. We also have some tips to keep you safe in Cambodian traffic.

Getting around by tuk tuk

The best way to travel around town in Cambodia is by tuk tuk. These tips will help you negotiate the price, stay safe, and get to your destination.

The tuk tuk has got to be one of the most pleasant forms of intraurban transit in Cambodia. These two-wheeled carriages pulled behind a moto are a breezy way to travel and are marginally safer than going by moto — mostly because they go at about half the speed.

Tuk tuks are also more expensive than motos, but worth the expense. Here are a few tips for taking tuk tuks:

Learn the pagodas and markets. Most tuk tuk drivers seem to have only a loose grasp of the geography of the area they work in and are not familiar with the sort of landmarks that Westerners generally use. For example, telling a tuk tuk driver a street name and cross street will often result in a blank stare. But tuk tuk drivers will almost always know the names of the local markets and pagodas (*wats*), so it's good to know which one you live closest to and give directions from there.

Negotiate the price in advance. When tuk tuk drivers see foreigners, they often see dollar signs floating over our heads. Therefore, it's better to negotiate a price in advance rather than risk having an argument about $2 in front of your house or the restaurant where you're having a business dinner. Negotiating a price in advance gives you the leverage to walk away if you don't think you're being offered a fair deal (and walking away usually drops the price substantially). Once you have a relationship with a regular driver, you can do as the locals do, and just pay what you think is fair at the end of the trip.

Negotiate in Khmer. This will almost always get you a better price. Remember, there are three levels of pricing in Cambodia: tourist, expat, and local. Knowing some basic Khmer will move you into the second category, at least. When you're new in town you'll almost always get the tourist price until you learn what a fair price is and how to bargain in Khmer. If you're offered a price that's too high, whine and say *"T'lai na!"* ("So expensive!"). Usually you'll be offered a better deal.

Don't go too low. If you've offered a price a few times and started to walk away and the tuk tuk driver doesn't bite, you're probably not offering enough. Tourists and new expats

LIVING

often start out by paying too much, and then overreact by trying to bargain down to a price that's much lower than what's really fair. Remember, the price of gasoline is almost certainly higher here than it is where you're from, so offering $1 for a ride all the way across town isn't realistic.

Scope out the drivers. Tuk tuk drivers who hang outside of hotels, bars, and clubs or speak English usually charge more than those who don't. Tuk tuk drivers who are on the move usually charge less than those who are sitting around waiting for a fare.

Get a map and learn to give directions in Khmer. This is perhaps the most crucial tip of all. Despite being transportation professionals, most tuk tuk drivers have no idea where your destination is, even if they tell you that they know. Expecting them to find it is usually an exercise in futility that will result in higher fares; after they get lost for 30 minutes they'll expect you to pay for the gas they expended driving in circles. You can find free Canby guides and maps in most of the tourist hotels and hot spots. Carry one with you when you travel, but don't expect drivers to be able to read it, since many are map-illiterate. Instead, learn the Khmer words for simple directions, which will help make your trip go more smoothly.

Here are some basic directions to help you get from here to there:

Turn right: *bot s'dam*
Turn left: *bot ch'wayng*
Go straight: *dtou dtrong*
Turn back: *dtou grao-ee*
Stop: *chop*

Stay safe. If you are in the back of a tuk tuk, you are at increased risk of having your bag snatched by young men on motos who make a sport of it. Make sure to hold your bag close to you, or keep it under your feet. Be alert when riding in tuk tuks. Those who who idly play with their expensive smartphones often find their expensive smartphones snatched out of their hands. Then they will probably wish they had signed up for travel insurance before coming to Cambodia.

Getting around by moto taxi

Taking a moto taxi — often called a *motodop* — is the cheapest, fastest way to get from point A to point B in Cambodia. But riding on the back of a motorcycle or scooter is also one of the easiest ways to get hurt in Cambodia.

Here are some tips for getting around Cambodia by moto taxi. Many of them are covered in more depth in the **Getting around by tuk tuk** section, but others are specific to moto taxis.

Get a map, learn the pagodas, and learn to give directions in Khmer. Always remember that most moto taxi drivers are not actually taxi drivers. They're just guys with motos who see a foreigner walking down the street and offer him a lift in exchange for cash. This means that if you take moto taxis you'll often meet off-duty police officers, teachers, and various other professionals. However, you'll rarely meet someone who has a working knowledge of the geography of the city you happen to be in, despite their assurances that they know exactly where you're going.

Remember that the Western frame of reference — using street names and cross streets — is foreign to most Cambodians, who use the locations of markets and pagodas

LIVING

(or *wats*) to help them navigate. Learning the names of the markets and pagodas closest to your destination will save you lots of time. Giving directions in Khmer will also make a big difference.

Stay safe. Driving laws in Cambodia are lax and the streets are unsafe. Moto accidents are Cambodia's leading cause of death, and countless expats are hurt every year because they've neglected to take elementary precautions while riding on motos.

If you choose to ride moto taxis, buy a helmet and put it on whenever you climb aboard a moto. (For more about helmets, see **Cambodian road safety**, on page 99.) Although moto drivers in Cambodia are required to wear helmets themselves, moto taxi drivers in Cambodia — unlike in many other countries — are not required to provide a helmet for their passengers (although new helmet laws are in the works).

This does not mean that you do not need to wear head protection. With or without laws requiring that you wear a helmet, your head is still just as likely to crack open like a melon when it hits the pavement. So please, wear a helmet. And make sure you have health insurance or travel insurance.

Another thing to remember is that many foreigners are targeted for bag-snatchings while riding on moto taxis. Ask the driver if he can hold your bag in front of him or if he can hook it to the moto. At least one tourist in Phnom Penh died when someone grabbed her bag and she was pulled off her moto and run over, and many others have been injured in similar incidents. If this makes you nervous, consider taking a tuk tuk or a car taxi.

Driving and traffic

New expats are often eager to hop onto their own moto and hit Cambodia's highways and byways. We can help you get a Cambodian driving license and get onto the road.

But be sure to be very careful—the roads in Cambodia are an adventure! There are the freewheeling (dare we say reckless?) drivers, of course, but also the police, who can seem to be waiting on every corner to exact a bribe. For those situations, we've got some tips for dealing with the police while you're on the road.

If you plan to own a car but don't want to drive yourself, you can learn more about hiring a driver in the **Hiring household staff** section (page 79).

Getting a Cambodian driving license

Foreigners who drive in Cambodia are legally required to have a Cambodian license. Many don't bother, and just pay (or avoid) the fines when they are stopped. But getting a driver's license in Cambodia isn't very difficult, and although the fines for driving without one are currently small, in the future the penalties for driving without a license will likely be more severe. Note that an International Driver's License is not recognized in Cambodia. Also note that if you get into an accident while driving without a valid Cambodian license, most health insurance and travel insurance companies will not cover your claim.

There are seven types of licenses in Cambodia. The non-industrial ones are:

A1: For 49-125cc motorcycles and scooters

A2: For motorcycles larger than 125cc

B: For passenger vehicles (less than 9 passengers)

License B also permits the holder to drive motorcycles under 125cc, but an A2 license is still required for larger motorcycles.

What you need to apply for a Cambodian driver's license:

- 3 passport photos

- Passport with current visa

- Valid driver's license from your home country

- Fee in US dollars, $35 (although agents may charge an additional fee)

Where to apply for a Cambodian driving license. To apply for a Cambodian driving license, you can do it the official way or use an agent.

The Department of Public Works and Transport can issue driver's licenses that are valid for one year for $35. The turnaround time is usually remarkably fast, sometimes just 24 hours. Five-year licenses are no longer available for foreigners.

The Department of Public Works and Transport
106 Preah Norodom Boulevard, Phnom Penh
Tel : 023 427 845; 023 427 862
www.mpwt.gov.kh

Most expats choose to not apply this way, however, and use an agent instead. The most popular agent for driver's licenses is Lucky! Lucky!, which also rents motos by the day or month. If you don't have a driving license from your home country, Lucky! Lucky! can also help you get set up with classes (if you'd like) for taking the test to get a Cambodian license.

Lucky! Lucky!
413 Monivong Boulevard, Phnom Penh
Tel: 023 220 988; 023 212 788; 099 808 788

Cambodian road safety

The streets and roads are the most dangerous parts of Cambodia, so expats should take extra precautions to stay safe while anywhere near traffic in the Kingdom of Wonder.

The thing to remember is that while you may have a Cambodian driver's license, many Cambodians do not. It's not uncommon to see tweens merrily driving along the roads, or to see five Cambodians piled onto a moto driven by an obviously intoxicated driver. It's wise to assume that everyone else on the road is drunk, distracted, or an awful driver—or all three.

Vehicular accidents are the leading cause of death in Cambodia, killing thousands every year. Of those who die, 77 percent are motorcycle drivers or passengers, and the cause of death is usually traumatic head injury. What does this mean? It means that if you choose to drive or ride a moto, you need to wear a helmet.

However, most helmets that are available in Cambodia are nearly worthless. The law states that all drivers must wear a helmet when driving a moto, so the helmets supplied are the cheapest possible, costing only a few dollars and providing about as much protection as a sun hat. This is one item to consider bringing from home.

Even if you get a good helmet, you'll still need to have some sort of insurance coverage as well. (For more on this topic, see the **Health insurance and travel insurance** section.) If you're in Cambodia on a temporary basis, you can get

LIVING

travel insurance. If you've moved for the long haul, get an expat insurance policy and make sure that you keep your insurance company's phone number with you at all times.

If you do get into an accident, consider contacting your embassy. They can help advocate for you and contact your loved ones.

US Embassy: For emergencies during business hours: Tel: 023 728 281; 023 728 051; 023 728 234. Outside of normal business hours: Tel: 023 728 000

UK Embassy: Tel: 023 427 124. Outside of normal business hours: Tel: 023 427 124; 023 428 153

Australia Embassy: Tel: 023 213 470

Dealing with the police

Most expats have at least a few run-ins with the police while driving in Cambodia, but if you know what to expect, it doesn't have to be a big deal.

On Twitter, the hashtag #myfirstbribe was briefly popular with expats who shared the first time they had to pay "tea money," the polite term for a bribe in Cambodia. Those stories generally involved driving.

What you have to remember is that the police, like many Cambodian government employees, don't make enough in salary to survive or to feed their families—they often get as little as $40 per month. This means they need to supplement their income in other ways. Many are moto taxi drivers when they are off-duty, and most believe that accepting bribes when dealing with those who have violated the law is acceptable.

As an expat, this can be hard to swallow. Fighting a bribe request may seem like the right thing to do, and perhaps it is, but it's also always the most complicated thing to do. Most expats have decided to look at it this way: at home, we pay lots of taxes and fees to make sure that our police officers are well paid. In Cambodia, we operate on a pay-per-service basis — meaning that you don't pay the police anything, until you need them.

While driving, you'll almost certainly be stopped for the crime of not being Cambodian. This will even more certainly happen to you if you drive in Sihanoukville, which is known for its overzealous traffic police. Police officers know that many foreigners have not bothered to obtain Cambodian licenses, so stopping them is an easy win. Another law that foreigners often break is driving with their lights on during the day. Yes, that's illegal (but driving with your lights off at night is not). You'll also need to have a copy of your vehicle registration and a yearly road tax sticker on your vehicle, which only costs a few bucks for motos but can be quite high for cars. If you don't have these, expect to be fined when you are stopped by the police.

What to do when you get stopped by the police

If you've broken the law, be prepared to pay a fine on the spot. Asking the police to write up paperwork and give you a ticket always costs much, much more and is not worth the hassle.

The days of gunning your moto and leaving the police in the dust are going the way of the Cambodian forests. That said, some foreigners do it, but it's not the smartest, or the safest, idea.

When stopped, take your keys out of the ignition immediately. The police will often take the keys from your ignition and refuse to give them back until you've paid a large sum. Savvy expats carry a spare set of keys with them.

This gives you more leverage in your negotiations. (And traffic fines are indeed negotiable.)

The same goes for your license and moto registration. It's much better to carry a color copy of your license and registration than the actual thing. Once you hand your license over to the police, they know it will cost you $35 to replace it and will try to ask for a $10 or $20 fine. Don't give them the opportunity.

Always carry 5,000 riel in your pocket when you are driving. If you whip out a wallet filled with $20 bills, your fine will end up being $20. Almost any infraction that does not involve hitting another vehicle can be negotiated down to between 5,000 and 10,000 riel. If they ask for more, pull the 5,000 riel out of your pocket and say that's all you have. Eventually, they will take it and let you go.

Be polite. Losing your temper never helps in Cambodia. Everything in Cambodia can be solved with money, and the police will usually let you go if you haven't done anything wrong. If you have—driving without a helmet or a license, or driving with your lights on—pay the fine with a smile and get on with your day.

Long-distance buses

If you're looking to travel around Cambodia, do as the locals do and hop on an inexpensive long-distance bus.

The buses in Cambodia are not the best in the world, but you'll be relieved to know that they're not the worst, either. There are around a dozen bus operators sending buses all over the country at any given time. Many are owned by the same companies and some have dubious safety records. The company with the best safety record is Mekong Express, which goes between Phnom Penh and Siem Reap. Rith Mony and Angkor Express have the worst safety records and are

Long haul

To travel to other cities, do like the locals do and take a bus.

best avoided. The rule of thumb is that you get what you pay for — the more expensive companies such as Mekong Express and Giant Ibis cater to tourists and have better safety records. Rith Mony, on the other hand, charges less but breaks down more often and packs many more people into each bus than there are seats.

These days most of the major roads are sealed, so the bus journeys are relatively short, with a trip between Phnom Penh and Siem Reap taking less than six hours.

There are also international routes going from Phnom Penh, Sihanoukville, and Siem Reap to Ho Chi Minh City (Saigon), Vietnam, and from Phnom Penh to Bangkok, to the Laos border via Strung Treng, and to the Thai border via Poipet.

Most buses in Cambodia play movies in various languages or Khmer television. It's likely that you'll also be treated to a few hours of Khmer karaoke videos, a true window into the culture of Cambodia. If this is a window you'd rather keep closed, bring a pair of ear plugs. Most buses are air-conditioned, often to an extreme, so bring a sweater as well. Some buses do have bathrooms on board, but most do not. The ones that don't will stop every hour or two at rest stations that have toilets—they are usually squat-style and do not have toilet paper, so bring some of your own if you require it. Rest stations also sell snacks, including fresh fruit, hard-boiled eggs, and prepared Khmer food. Each stop will last 10 to 20 minutes, but keep your eye on the bus, as the driver won't necessarily notice if you haven't made it back to your seat before he takes off.

The night buses in Cambodia are not recommended, as they seem to be very prone to accidents. Overall, though, the buses in Cambodia are a pleasant and inexpensive way to see the country.

The **Canby Guide** has a good summary of domestic and international bus routes in Cambodia (www.canbypublications.com/cambodia/buses.htm), although be sure to check with the bus operators, as they do change regularly.

Flights

Within Cambodia there are limited flights between Siem Reap and Phnom Penh and Siem Reap and Sihanoukville. These flights are generally quite expensive, and most expats opt for a private taxi or long-distance bus instead.

Both Phnom Penh and Siem Reap have international airports that host a number of airlines.

**In Phnom Penh,
these airlines offer flights to the following cities:**

Air France: Paris
AirAsia: Bangkok, Kuala Lumpur
Asiana Airlines: Seoul
Bangkok Airways: Bangkok
Cambodia Angkor Air: Ho Chi Minh City, Siem Reap
Cathay/Dragonair: Hong Kong
China Airlines: Taipei
China Eastern Airlines: Kunming, Nanning
China Southern Airlines: Beijing, Guangzhou
EVA Air: Taipei
Jetstar: Singapore
Korean Air: Seoul
Lao Airlines: Vientiane
Malaysia Airlines: Kuala Lumpur
Shanghai Airlines: Shanghai
SilkAir: Singapore
Thai Airways: Bangkok
Tiger Airways: Singapore
Vietnam Airlines: Hanoi, Ho Chi Minh City, Vientiane

LIVING

These airlines fly to the following cities from Siem Reap

AirAsia: Kuala Lumpur
Asiana Airlines: Seoul
Bangkok Airways: Bangkok
Cambodia Angkor Air: Ho Chi Minh City, Phnom
    Penh, Sihanoukville
Cebu Pacific: Manila
China Eastern Airlines: Shanghai, Kunming
China Southern Airlines: Guangzhou
Jetstar: Singapore
Korean Air: Busan, Seoul

Lao Airlines: Luang Prabang, Pakse, Vientiane
Malaysia Airlines: Kuala Lumpur
Myanmar Airways International: Phnom Penh, Yangon
Skywings Asia Airlines: Seoul, Hanoi
Singapore/SilkAir: Da Nang, Singapore
Tonlesap Airlines: Ningbo, Kaohsiung, Taipei
Vietnam Airlines: Hanoi, Ho Chi Minh City,
     Luang Prabang

For some reason, many of these airlines forget to include Cambodia on their web sites. If you can't book a ticket directly, it's often useful to go to a flight aggregator such as Expedia. Last year Cambodia folded its $25 departure tax into the price of flights leaving the country, so you won't need to pay any additional fees on your way out.

Religious organizations and worship

Even though almost all of Cambodia practices Theravada Buddhism, on the whole the locals are remarkably tolerant toward other religions and those who practice them. There are expats of all stripes here, practicing just about all of the major religions in many languages. Like the expat community itself, much of this religious activity is centered in Phnom Penh, but there are religious groups and missionary organizations all over the country. If you're looking for information outside of Phnom Penh, considering contacting the most relevant group below to find out what's available in your area.

The Church of Christ Our Peace (Anglican)
57 Street 294 (between Norodom Blvd. and Street 51), Phnom Penh
Mailing address: PO Box 1413, Phnom Penh, Cambodia
Tel: 023 217 429
Email: aeccadm@online.com.kh
Part of the Anglican Church of Cambodia (ACC), the Church of Christ Our Peace has weekly services on Sunday in English at 10 a.m. and youth group activities. The congregation is small but friendly, with a traditional Anglican service.

International Christian Fellowship of Phnom Penh
ICF Centre
19/21 Street 330, Phnom Penh
Tel: 098 512 211
Email: admin@icfpp.org
www.icfpp.org

The ICF calls itself "an international, interdenominational, English-speaking, independent Christian church" and is popular with expats. In addition to Sunday services, this evangelical organization offers home groups, prayer groups, and fellowship and social events.

Chabad Cambodia
32 Street 228, Phnom Penh
Tel: 085 807 205
www.jewishcambodia.com
According to Chabad Cambodia, there are more than 100 Jewish people living in the country, with 70 of them in Phnom Penh. The center offers synagogue services, Friday night dinner, kosher food, adult education, a Jewish library, and special high holiday events.

Church of Jesus Christ of Latter-Day Saints
267 Street 63, Phnom Penh
Tel: 023 994 171
Although there are many Mormon churches in Phnom Penh and wider Cambodia, most serve locals rather than expats. The Street 63 church in Phnom Penh is the LDS international branch, and they have English-language services between 10 a.m. and 1 p.m. every Sunday.

International Baptist Church
103 Norodom Bvld. at the corner of Street 222, Phnom Penh
Tel: 092 723 350
The International Baptist Church has services in English at 10 a.m. every Sunday. (Services in Khmer are at 8 a.m. and 6 p.m.)

Life Bible Presbyterian English Church

Life University

Group II, Mondol 3, Sangkat 2, Sihanoukville

Email: lifeenglishchurch@gmail.com

lifeenglishchurch.wordpress.com

One of Sihanoukville's only English-language churches, Life Bible Presbyterian English Church offers services on the grounds of Life University. Most of the worshippers are university students, but locals, expats, and tourists are all welcome. English-language services are held Sundays at 10 a.m. Khmer services are held at the same time and Korean-language services are held at 8:30 a.m. on Sundays. On the first Sunday of each month combined services are held at 10 a.m. on the fourth floor.

Catholic Cambodia

The first Catholic missionaries came to Cambodia in 1555, and they're still here! There are now Catholic churches in eight of Cambodia's provinces and in 83 communities. The Catholic Cambodia website (www.catholiccambodia.org/home/en) is a good resource for more detailed information.

Chapel of the Missionaries of Charity

475 Boulevard Monivong, Phnom Penh

Tel: 023 213 491

An English-language Catholic mass is held every day except Saturday.

LIVING

World Vision Cambodia
20 Street 71, Phnom Penh
Tel: 023 216 052
Every Saturday at 5 p.m. an English-language Catholic
service is held at the Phnom Penh headquarters of the World
Vision Christian humanitarian organization.

St. John's Church
Riverside Road, Slorgram Village, Group I, No 027, Slorgram
    Commune, Siem Reap
Tel: 012 661 747
In Siem Reap, there are English-language Catholic services
on Saturdays at 6:30 p.m.

Love and family

From dating to sex to families, we've got
the scoop.

**Cambodia is relaxed about many things, including
foreigners' sex lives — most of the time. But it's wise
to learn what's regarded as acceptable and what isn't,
whether you're dating across gender lines or paired off
with a same-sex partner. For those who've moved on to
the next phase of life, we've got information for parents
on raising kids in Cambodia, plus advice on education and
international schools.**

Sex and dating

Sex and dating are complicated topics in Cambodia, perhaps
because the country is only in the first stages of what may
turn out to be a full-scale sexual revolution.

Traditionally, Cambodian girls are quite conservative.
There's an old Cambodian proverb that says, "Women are
like white cloth and men are like gold. If you drop a piece
of gold in the mud, it can be cleaned. But if you drop white
cloth in the mud, it is stained forever." This of course refers
to virginity and the fact that in traditional Cambodian
culture women's virtue is very highly valued.

On the other hand, Cambodia has one of the world's
highest percentages of both married and unmarried men
who utilize the services of prostitutes. So it's fair to say that
Cambodia is a place that is not particularly accepting of
female sexuality but at the same time gives men free rein to
do whatever they want.

And while most Cambodians do subscribe to the belief that a woman's virginity is her highest virtue, there are many women who live outside of the traditional framework. Women who are divorced or have had premarital sex are considered "ruined" by Cambodian culture, and they often end up working in the sex industry. Others look to date foreign men who will not hold their pasts against them. And more young, urban middle-class women are rejecting the idea that their mothers should choose their suitors or that they should wait for marriage to become romantically involved with their partners.

Male expats who move to Cambodia generally find themselves an object of desire in a way they have never previously experienced, a situation that many find difficult to resist. It's true that many Cambodian women are willing to overlook qualities that are important in the West — age, weight, looks, etc. — in exchange for financial stability. It's also true that they may be searching for said financial stability in more than one wallet, while also keeping a much-loved Cambodian boyfriend on the side.

The phenomenon of "professional girlfriends" is very prevalent in Cambodia: a local woman will fulfill a girlfriend role in an expat's life in exchange for financial remuneration. While this may not be outright prostitution, it can have a more overtly mercenary flavor than the typical Western love relationship. Often the expat will not be aware that his girlfriend sees him as more business than pleasure, which can lead to a lot of misunderstandings and hurt feelings.

That's not to say there aren't sweet, lovely Cambodians willing to date Westerners without a financial incentive. But many expats have found that if it seems too good to be true, it might just be. (The same is true in the gay community as well.)

Female expats, on the other hand, generally tend not to take on Khmer suitors (although there are a few success stories of those who did and have ended up happy ever after). This creates an unbalanced hetero dating scene among expats. Those expat men who prefer to date Western women are also likely to find that their company is in much greater demand than it was at home, and most are thrilled to take advantage of that fact.

A few years ago the female experience of dating in Cambodia's expat community could readily be compared to fishing in a polluted pond. Few expat men were untainted by at least one run-in with a local prostitute, and the female-to-male ratio was wildly unbalanced, a situation that allowed mostly undesirable men to call all the shots. These days, though, the male-to-female ratio has improved, Cambodia is becoming a destination of choice for bright young professionals, and many expats have met their partners within the foreign community.

Moreover, within the growing and educated Cambodian middle class, especially in Phnom Penh, young people are starting to reject traditional values and forge their own paths, which sometimes intersect romantically with an expat.

Gay culture

Same same, but different: Cambodia is very accepting of gay culture and gay expats. While there aren't any official laws on the books in Cambodia protecting the rights of the LGBT community, same-sex sexual activity is legal and accepted. (Commercial sex acts are prohibited, as they are between opposite-sex partners.)

The culture is so accepting of LGBTs, in fact, that business owners recently launched a tourism campaign to attract more gay visitors to the Kingdom, and specifically

LIVING

INTERVIEW WITH AN EXPAT

What's the gay scene like in Phnom Penh?

The highlight is the weekend shows at the gay bars, which are great fun and bring together expats and tourists as well as the local Cambodian gay crowd. These bars are not for the faint-hearted, though, and there are a lot of Cambodian 'moneyboys' who may be trying to pick up people with ulterior motives. Heart of Darkness usually has a diverse crowd and there is above-average representation from the gay community (who head here after the bars close).

These bars aside, I think most people here would agree that the social scene, both Khmer and expat, is fairly mixed, with a lot of gay-friendly and gay-owned venues. There is also a Khmer-orientated gay scene that most Westerners may not be aware of, headed by organizations like M-Style and clubs like Classic.

How is gay culture changing in Cambodia?

I think traditionally there has been a lot of ignorance of the kind of "gay identity" that we are so used to in the West. Same-sex relationships have always existed here, and they are free of the usual religiously fueled prejudice common elsewhere. However, there has always been pressure to marry and have children, regardless of sexual preference.

to Siem Reap, where many hotels and businesses enthusiastically welcome gay men.

Gay culture in both Phnom Penh and Siem Reap is rich; clubs, bars, and hotels catering to gay expats and tourists are all over the place. In Phnom Penh, Blue Chili, 2 Colors, Rainbow Bar, Shameless on Thursdays at Pontoon, the Empire, and the Local 2 are all gay-owned or gay-friendly. In Siem Reap, Linga Bar, Miss Wong, and the Station Wine Bar are all gay-owned or gay-friendly. Many hotels in Siem Reap,

There aren't really words that accurately reflect the terms "gay" and "lesbian" in Khmer, as they are not really seen as identities. The closest is *katoey*, which refers to the Thai-style third sex and is used for transgender 'ladyboys' and intersex. As organizations seek to educate people on sexual identity and events like Cambodia Pride continue to grow, this is changing. But it's more about awareness and education than challenging people's prejudices.

What's it like being in a same-sex relationship in Cambodia? How are you and your partner treated?

It's actually very easy to be in a same-sex relationship. The only hints of homophobia I've noticed here have been from Westerners. I'm in a relationship with a Cambodian, and the bigger issue for us has been with cultural difference, as I imagine it would be in a cross-cultural heterosexual relationship. Sexual identity and gender politics aside, life is generally very easygoing for same-sex couples here, so long as you respect cultural differences (things like open displays of affection, etc.), which would be the case for most people. It's true to say that I feel more comfortable and free of prejudice being in a same-sex relationship here then I would back in the UK.

Niall Crotty
owner, The Empire
www.the-empire.org

including the Golden Banana, MEN's Resort and Spa, and Cockatoos, cater to the LGBT crowd.

Same-sex relationships between Khmers and foreigners are tolerated, although these couples are expected to forego canoodling in public, just like their heterosexual peers. However, same-sex friends will often walk hand-in-hand, and it doesn't mean that they are gay.

While same-sex sexual activity among Khmers is accepted, most Cambodian men who have sex with men do not identify as homosexual and also have female partners or wives, due to the strong societal pressure to marry and have children. Even after marriage, however, men often continue to engage in same-sex sexual activity, and HIV rates among these men and their female partners are quite high, around 9 percent.

In Khmer culture, the word *katoey* denotes a third gender. It is often used to describe "ladyboys" but is also used for homosexuals of all stripes, and when used in the latter sense it's considered derogatory. Generally *katoey* are accepted or at the least tolerated; hair and makeup salons run by *katoey* are quite popular with Khmer women, who flock there when they want to look their best. However, *katoeys* can still face discrimination in Cambodia. Khmer lesbians seem to face even more discrimination, perhaps because of their increasing unwillingness to enter into sham marriages to men.

Every May Cambodia LGBT Pride holds a week-long pride event, where they work to reduce discrimination and celebrate LGBT contributions to the Cambodian community.

For more info, visit: www.facebook.com/cambodiapride.

Expat kids in Cambodia

While some may balk at moving to Cambodia with children, those who have find that it's a great place for families. Babies and children, especially the pale-skinned Western variety, are treated very well in Cambodia. It's not uncommon for restaurant waitstaff to offer to mind your baby or toddler while you eat, because they're so delighted to meet a foreign child. Blond, blue-eyed tots will quickly grow used to random Cambodians squawking appreciatively at them in the street and pinching their cheeks.

Nannies are inexpensive (see the **Hiring household staff** section, page 79), meaning that there's no need for daycare. Moreover, this gives kids the opportunity to become multilingual.

In Phnom Penh particularly, there are indoor and outdoor playgrounds all over town—check out Wat Botum park, Dreamland, City Mall, Sorya Mall, and Pencil Riverside.

Also, stores catering to children have been popping up all over the place, offering a range of children's toys and clothing that would have been hard to imagine here a few years ago.

Monument Books in Phnom Penh and Siem Reap sell a good selection of educational toys and children's books, as well as educational publications for teaching purposes.

The **Cambodia Parent Network** (groups.yahoo.com/group/cambodiaparentnetwork) is a great resource for parents who want to learn more about what it's like bringing kids to Cambodia and other issues pertaining to parents and children.

LIVING

Schools in Cambodia

While it's true that schools in Cambodia aren't the best, there are a few international schools using American, British, and French curricula. Don't be fooled by the names, though; some of the worst schools in the country call themselves "international" or "American" or "British," but their curricula don't match the titles.

The two big international schools in Phnom Penh, **Northbridge** (www.nisc.edu.kh) and **ISPP** (www.ispp.edu.kh), are accredited abroad, offering International Baccalaureate programs. While their curricula and teachers are the best, they cost upwards of $10,000 per year and there is said to be a "brat pack" feeling of privilege among the students.

Also popular with expats is the slightly less expensive **iCAN British International School** (www.ican.edu.kh), which teaches a British curriculum, and the **Lycée**

Descartes (www.descartes-cambodge.com), a private French school offering international-quality education in English and French.

In Phnom Penh, **Footprints** (www.footprintsschool.edu.kh) is a popular school for expats not looking to break the bank. Footprints offers a bilingual program from nursery classes to grade 5. And there are definitely many other less costly, good-quality schools in town.

In Siem Reap the options are more limited. **ISSR** (www.issr-cambodia.com) offers classes to grade 9. The **Ecole Francaise de Siem Reap** (www.ecolefr-siemreap.org) offers classes in French but does admit non-French-speaking children up to age six.

Outside of Phnom Penh and Siem Reap, expat parents often join together to create educational programs for young learners, pooling together to hire international and local teachers or using homeschooling curricula. Many believe that the experience of living abroad is invaluable to youngsters and that its advantages outweigh those of a formal classroom setting.

INTERVIEW WITH AN EXPAT

How have you dealt with educating your young daughter in Cambodia?

Because we are not living in an area hugely populated by expats and therefore don't have access to international schools, we started up our own playgroup with a group of other like-minded parents, which over time has naturally grown into a preschool. The school is run by a parents' cooperative, which of course can be tricky at times (it's a lot of unpaid work, parents have different opinions), but also extremely rewarding, as we are highly involved in and aware of how our daughter is being educated. She has the benefit of being exposed to children from a variety of backgrounds, and because there is a lower student-to-teacher ratio, lessons and activities can be carefully geared to suit specific needs. All that being said, we have no idea what the future will hold, so in terms of planning we have to be very open-minded for any possibility.

Lindsay Oliver
mother of two

What factors helped you decide which of the international schools to send your children to?

The schools have differences in facilities and access, but none so significant that it would sway our decision on its own. At the end of the day, for lower grades it mostly comes down to which teacher your kid gets assigned, and it's mostly random chance. Get a good one and you're happy, otherwise. . .

We're moving now to Chiang Mai [in Thailand] almost entirely because the international schools there are of significantly higher quality in respect to facilities, and the living situation there offers more alternatives for older kids.

Jeffrey Himel
father of two

LIVING

Health and medical care

One challenge for potential expats is the state of Cambodia's health-care system. Truth be told, it's not the greatest!

While Cambodian health care can leave a lot to be desired, there's no need to get discouraged. We'll give you some tips on getting medical care in Cambodia (and when to leave to get care elsewhere), as well as the best options for taking care of your teeth and your eyesight. We cover ailments in Cambodia and women's health plus recommend the best doctors and hospitals in the country. We can also help you find trustworthy pharmacies and decide whether you should buy health insurance or travel insurance.

Common ailments

It's surprisingly easy to stay healthy in Cambodia (if you choose to), but there are always things to watch out for.

Food poisoning. Rare are the expats who make it through their first few months in-country without at least one round of food poisoning or serious case of diarrhea. Instead of fearing it, embrace it—it's a great weight-loss technique! Seriously, it's nearly unavoidable, even for those who spend their time here avoiding local food and fussing about whether or not they can have a beverage with ice in it. Instead of limiting your experience in Cambodia, accept the inevitable. It won't last long. And luckily, there's no shortage of Pepto-Bismol and Imodium in the country.

Mosquitos. One of the things to be most aware of in Cambodia is mosquitos. Dengue fever has been on the rise, especially during and just after the wet season, even in the cities, and there are no vaccinations to prevent it. Malaria is also present (mostly in rural locales and near forested areas), but most expats make the decision that being on anti-malarial drugs for extended periods of time is not worth it. This means that preventing mosquito bites is key. Wear long-sleeved shirts if possible, use a DEET-containing mosquito repellent, and sleep with closed windows or a mosquito net.

Worms. Another affliction long-term expats often encounter is invasion by various types of intestinal worms. Although you'll probably know it if you have them (tell-tale signs are an itchy butt or actually seeing the worms), some recommend taking anti-worm medication every six months just to be safe. The medication is called mebendazole. It can be found at any pharmacy in Cambodia and costs around 2,000 riel.

Heat rash. Prickly heat or heat rash is another common complaint. Although not serious, heat rash can be annoying; the itchy red rash on the body causes a pins-and-needles sensation. It's common in hot, humid environments and occurs when sweat is trapped beneath the skin. The easiest way to avoid heat rash is to shower often and avoid sweating too much, especially in fabrics that don't breathe. Particularly when you first arrive, don't be afraid to turn on the air-conditioning! Prickly heat powder is available in all pharmacies and can help relieve symptoms.

STDs. Sexually transmitted infections are also common in Cambodia's expat population, particularly among those who favor the services of sex workers. It's important to always use a condom. Local brands OK and Number 1 are released by

LIVING

PSI, an NGO, and meet international standards. Durex is also available at U-Care pharmacy.

Almost all of the above ailments are contracted through carelessness, so be alert to the risks and take care of your health while you're in Cambodia.

The state of medical care

One good reason to safeguard your health is that the medical care available in Cambodia leaves a lot to be desired. But it's getting better with each passing day. Still, for serious conditions (and many not-so-serious ones) expats who can afford it generally choose to seek medical care in Bangkok or Singapore.

Most expats would agree that Khmer doctors who have been trained in Cambodia are best avoided. Many are practicing without any sort of certification that would be recognized outside of the country and do not offer services that would meet international standards.

However, there are also many Khmer doctors who have been trained abroad, and they offer services for far less than those charged by most foreign doctors working in Cambodia. Expats give mixed reports of these doctors — some offer very good medical care for a song, others. . . well, do not.

While Cambodia has a number of reputable hospitals and doctors, nevertheless it's best to make sure you have health insurance that will cover you for medical evacuation in case you need to leave the country for care.

Hospitals

Phnom Penh. In Phnom Penh, Thai-owned Royal Rattanak Hospital is the best international hospital in town, but it's not cheap! You can see Khmer doctors there for less than the foreign doctors charge, but it's still fairly pricey. A less expensive option that expats still trust is Sen Sok University Hospital.

Royal Rattanak Hospital
11 Street 592, Toul Kork, Phnom Penh
Tel: 023 991 000; 023 365 555
www.royalrattanakhospital.com

Sen Sok International University Hospital
91-96 Street 1986, Phnom Penh
Tel: 023 883 712; 012 840 731
www.sensokiuh.com

Siem Reap. In Siem Reap the options are even more limited. Royal Angkor International Hospital is the best available, but that isn't saying much. If you are traveling with children, you can see someone at the Angkor Hospital for Children in Siem Reap, but expect a long wait.

Royal Angkor International Hospital
National Route 6 (Airport Road), Siem Reap
Tel: 063 761 888; 012 235 888; 063 399 111
www.royalangkorhospital.com

Angkor Hospital for Children
Tep Vong (Achamean) Road and Oum Chhay Street,
    Siem Reap
Tel: 063 963 409
angkorhospital.org

LIVING

Kampot. In Kampot a new hospital, Sonja Kill Memorial, has recently been opened by a group of German foundations and Hope Worldwide, and it is said to be state of the art. While the hospital's mission is to help children and expectant mothers, it will also treat expats (and not just of the mother-and-child variety). Patients are charged on a sliding scale, and foreigners are expected to pay $20 for an consultation with a Western doctor.

Sonja Kill Memorial Hospital
National Road 3 (6km west of Kampot, close to the road to
    Bokor mountain), Kampot
Tel: 012 738 888; 092 210 599
www.skmh.org

Doctors and clinics

Phnom Penh. The only true international clinic in Phnom Penh, International SOS, offers a wide range of services at prices you'd expect to pay back home—they subsidize care for wealthy locals by charging expats significantly more. They do offer fairly good care, but expats suggest that you're better off seeing one of their foreign doctors.

International SOS Cambodia
161 Street 51, Phnom Penh
Tel: 023 216 911; 012 816 911
www.internationalsos.com/en/asia-pacific_cambodia.htm

Dr. Scott at Travellers Medical Clinic is another expat favorite in Phnom Penh. Dr. Scott, an Englishman, has been practicing medicine in Cambodia for more than 20 years and is the doctor of choice for tropical and sexually transmitted diseases.

Travellers Medical Clinic
88 Street 108 (Wat Phnom Quarter), Phnom Penh
Tel: 023 306 802; 012 898 981
www.travellersmedicalclinic.com

Siem Reap. In Siem Reap the best of the bunch seems to be Naga Clinic, where they have doctors who speak Dutch, German, English, and French as well as some Swedish and Khmer. Many expats in Siem Reap choose to take a taxi to Phnom Penh when they really need care.

Naga Clinic Siem Reap
660 Hup Guan Street (behind Central Market), Siem Reap
Tel: 092 793 180; 063 761 295; 012 363 601
www.nagahealthcare.com

Sihanoukville. Although the health care in Sihanoukville could best be described as subpar, the clinic that expats choose is CT Clinic, where an English doctor is employed.

CT Clinic
47 Borei Kamakor Street, Sihanoukville
Tel: 081 886 666

Pharmacies and medicine

All medications are sold over the counter in Cambodia. However, that includes many counterfeit drugs. So it's best to head to a reputable pharmacy, although they do cost more than the local pharmacies. The chain that everyone seems to trust is U-Care, located in Phnom Penh and Siem Reap. Additionally, Pharmacie De La Gare in Phnom Penh has a good reputation.

LIVING

You should be able to find most popular medications in Cambodia, particularly in Phnom Penh or Siem Reap. If you have a prescription for a specific medication, it's worth calling U-Care before you move to make sure that they carry it or will be able to order it for you. Some medications are not yet available in the Kingdom and others, including many that are restricted in the United States, such as ADHD medications, are not available at all.

U-Care Pharmacy
39 Sihanouk Boulevard, Phnom Penh
Tel: 023 224 299

U-Care Pharmacy
Hospital Street, at Pub Street, Siem Reap
Tel: 063 965 396 (Ex. 104)
Visit their site for a list of all branches:
www.u-carepharmacy.com

Pharmacie De La Gare
81 Monivong Boulevard, Phnom Penh
Tel: 023 430 205; 012 805 908

Women's health

Women will find that most of their health needs are covered in Cambodia.

Tampons. Tampons are available in the major cities, although finding them in the countryside is unlikely—most Cambodian women do not use them. Menstrual cups are not currently available.

Contraceptives. Oral contraceptives are available in Cambodia, but often under different names than the ones at home. They will have the same formulas, but the brands can differ from country to country. The medications available in Cambodia come from around the world, often Australia, France, Thailand, and the United States. It's best to write down your specific brand's dose of estrogen and/or progesterone, take it to U-Care Pharmacy, and find the equivalent.

Finding progesterone-only birth control pills in Cambodia can be a challenge. Currently the patch, ring, and diaphragm are not sold here.

The depo injection and implant are popular with Cambodian women and are easy to find, as are copper IUDs. At the time of writing there are no clinics offering hormonal IUDs, so expats must go to Thailand to get one.

Abortion. Abortions have been legal in Cambodia since 1997 up until 12 weeks of pregnancy. After 12 weeks the law restricts abortions to certain situations. Currently abortions are not legal in Thailand except under certain circumstances, but legal up to 24 weeks in Singapore. However, Singapore does restrict abortions for non-residents.

Birthing and maternity. Most expats who are starting a family choose to give birth in Thailand at Samitivej or Bumrungrad hospital, and usually spend the few weeks or months before and after there as well. However, as medical care in Phnom Penh steadily improves, many expats are choosing to give birth in the capital. There are a few Western doulas, midwives, and obstetricians working in Cambodia who can help you through the entire process.

Lindsay Oliver has written a very informative rundown of her recent experience having a

LIVING

baby in Thailand (www.talesfromanexpat.com/
how-to-have-a-baby-in-bangkok-expat-style/).

Cambodia Parent Network is the best place to get up-to-date information on maternity issues and the latest new clinics (groups.yahoo.com/group/cambodiaparentnetwork/).

PERSPECTIVE

Birthing in Bangkok

We decided to have our second baby in Bangkok for a couple of reasons: it was less expensive than taking the whole family home to Canada for three months (renting a house, car, paying for flights, etc.), and also we liked the idea of not having to travel so far from home (and not having to be away for so long). And it would have been freezing in December in Canada!

I had my 12-week scan in Phnom Penh at the maternity clinic on Kampuchea Krom. It's the same place I went for my ultrasounds with our daughter, and it is fantastic — I think this time the cost had gone up from $10 to $12. They have extremely modern machines (much better than any scans I've ever had in Canada or France), you don't need to make an appointment, and they can tell you the gender of your baby at this first scan (normally you have to wait until your 20-week scan).

I was going back to Canada anyway, so had my bloodwork done there this time, but last time I had it done at a local clinic in Sihanoukville with no problems. Other than that, I got no prenatal care at all until we got to Bangkok when I was eight months along. We were fortunate that there were no issues, but there are certainly places you can go in Phnom Penh if concerns arise, or in Bangkok for anything serious.

Lindsay Oliver
Kampot expat

Dental care

While expats shrink from getting medical care in Cambodia, most will concede that the dental care is quite good, and very reasonably priced. There are a number of international dentists working here, and even more Cambodian dentists who have been trained abroad.

In Phnom Penh, expats favor the European Dental Clinic and the Roomchang Dental Hospital. Surprisingly enough, European Dental has actual European dentists. Cleanings there cost $40. Roomchang dentists are foreign-trained Khmers, and a check-up and cleaning costs $20.

European Dental Clinic
160A Norodom Boulevard, Phnom Penh
Tel: 023 211 363; 012 893 174
Emergencies: 092 804 471; 012 986 024
www.europeandentalclinic-asia.com

Roomchang Dental Hospital
4 Street 184, Phnom Penh
Tel: 023 211 338
Emergencies: 011 811 338
www.roomchang.com

In Siem Reap, the best choice is Pachem Dental Clinic, where a cleaning will set you back $15 and a root canal costs about $50.

Pachem Dental Clinic
242 Mondul, Siem Reap District
Tel: (063) 96 53 33; (013) 83 83 03
www.pachemdental.com

Eye care

For those not blessed with perfect vision, Cambodia has positives and negatives. On the downside, expats complain that their eyes and contact lenses are easily irritated by the large amounts of dust and dirt in the air, especially in the provinces. On the plus side, glasses are cheaper in Cambodia than what you'll pay at home. However, for anything more than the basics, many expats choose to seek care in Thailand or Vietnam.

Ophthalmologists. Dr. Do Seiha is generally considered the best ophthalmologist in Cambodia. He trained in Russia and Australia and speaks fluent English. Dr. Do works at the Phnom Penh Naga Clinic during the day, but sees patients at his private practice in the evenings after 5 p.m. Appointments cost around $10.

Dr. Do Seiha
#121 Street 110, Phnom Penh
Tel: 012 840 796

Glasses. If you wear glasses, you'll find that plastic lenses are easily scratched by the dust in Cambodia. Get glass lenses or non-scratch plastic ones.

Thailand has a better range of frames than Cambodia (and they usually cost 10 to 20 percent less), so consider getting frames when you're in Bangkok. You can also buy frames at Central Market in Phnom Penh for less than they'd cost at the shops, although there are also fewer guarantees about quality.

Here are a few recommended opticians in Phnom Penh and Siem Reap:

Poly Optics
#17 Street 13, Phnom Penh
Tel: 016 525 346; 011 750 685

Grand Optics
11 Norodom Boulevard (at Street 154), Phnom Penh
Tel: 023 213 585; 011 740 750; 012 848 516

King Optics
7 Sivatha Street, Siem Reap
Tel: 012 778 286; 016 648 191; 010 396 754

Angkor Optics
Canadia Business Center, Sivatha Street, Siem Reap
Tel: 063 761 237; 017 974 726

Contact lenses. You can find standard brands of contact lenses, such as Acuvue, in Cambodia, often priced lower than they are at home because they're manufactured for the Asian market. You also have the option of purchasing generics. Monthly contact lenses are widely available. However, toric lenses are not sold in Cambodia (although they can be found in Bangkok).

In Phnom Penh and Siem Reap, most optics stores tend to have the same prices for contact lenses. You just need to find one that carries your specific prescription.

Local pharmacies generally do not carry contact lens solution, but you can find it at any of the **U-Care pharmacies** (www.u-carepharmacy.com). The optical stores also sell it.

Health insurance and travel insurance

Health insurance is a topic that some expats try to ignore. Many who abhor the idea of the "nanny state" end up in

Cambodia and, sticking to their guns, choose not to purchase insurance. It's only when they end up in the hospital after getting into a moto accident that they learn the folly of their ways.

While Cambodia is not a very dangerous place, its roads are. And while basic medical care is quite inexpensive, there are many procedures that no one who cares about his health should have done here, and medical evacuation is very, very expensive. If you're not insured for it, expect to spend upwards of $20,000 if you need to be airlifted to Singapore—and your transporters will expect to be paid up front.

Many expats get by using only travel insurance. For those who are in Cambodia for a short period of time and who have a national health-care system at home, this is a reasonable choice. Travel insurance is much cheaper than expat health insurance, primarily because it will usually only cover enough care to stabilize you. For example, if you're in a serious car accident, travel insurance will cover your acute-care hospital bills but won't cover the months of rehabilitation you'll need. They will, however, send you home, so for those who have some kind of coverage in their home country, travel insurance can be a good option.

The most flexible policy available is provided by **World Nomads** (www.worldnomads.com). They offer excellent options for those who claim Cambodia as their country of residence (as well as for those residing outside the country and just visiting).

If you're moving to Cambodia long term, a better option is to get real health insurance. Two of the most popular policies are Aetna Global Benefits and April Asia Expat. When you're deciding whether or not you need to get a comprehensive plan, remember that it's quite easy to get admitted to the hospital in Cambodia—being willing to pay the bill is enough to get you hospitalized for minor procedures.

Aetna Global Benefits, based in the United States, offers worldwide comprehensive plans that, while expensive, get consistently high ratings. They'll cover you in your home country, including the United States. They have options that are for hospital care only, or comprehensive plans that cover outpatient care as well.

April International, a French company, offers an insurance policy specifically designed for expats of all nationalities living in Asia. They have a basic option that covers medical and maternity care, and a comprehensive plan that includes hospital, maternity, and routine health care and dental care as well. For an additional $292 per year, they will also cover medical evacuation and repatriation. They do not cover any care in the United States, Japan, and Switzerland, so if you are from one of these countries consider getting a supplemental World Nomads travel insurance policy when you vacation in your home country.

French insurance broker David Treal of AG Associates in Phnom Penh offers his services in French and English and can help you pick the most appropriate expat policy for your specific situation.

AG Associates
313 Sisowath Quay, Hotel Cambodiana, office No 3,
    Phnom Penh
Tel: 023 998 018
www.agcambodia.com

Aetna International
www.aetnainternational.com

April International
www.aprilmobilite.com/assurance/site/fr/lang/en/accueil

LIVING

Getting medical care outside of Cambodia

Although many expats are satisfied with the medical care they can obtain in Cambodia, there are also many who are not. Expectant mothers frequently choose to deliver outside of Cambodia, and those who have serious medical problems also often decide to go elsewhere for care. Even if you just need certain simple office procedures or medical tests, these services may not be available in Cambodia, or if they are the prices can be quite high. So often it makes sense to seek care outside of the country, usually in Bangkok or Singapore.

Bangkok

Bangkok luxury hospital Bumrungrad offers many package deals for those coming from overseas, starting with a comprehensive check-up ranging in price from $79 to $265, maternity packages, and plastic surgery, too. If you need to stay overnight for outpatient care, they have a posh hotel on site. Those who are admitted as inpatients also get plush accommodations; the rooms at Bumrungrad are ridiculously nice, featuring WiFi, on-demand movies, and takeout Thai food. It's one of the most expensive hospitals in Bangkok, but still low cost compared to what it would be in most Western countries.

Bangkok's Samitivej Sukhumvit Hospital is another popular choice with expats. It offers excellent care and all of the staff speak English. Package deals are on offer here as well. A basic check-up package costs $210 and is a bit richer than Bumrungrad's, with a menu that includes chest X-ray, EKG, abdominal ultrasound, and a battery of blood tests. Samitivej is also a very fancy hospital, but perhaps not aimed so squarely at overseas expats as Bumrungrad is. However, by many accounts they offer superior care.

For eye complaints and surgery, many expats go to Rutnin Eye Hospital.

Bumrungrad International Hospital
33 Sukhumvit 3, Wattana, Bangkok 10110, Thailand
Tel: +66 2 667 1000
www.bumrungrad.com/

Samitivej Sukhumvit Hospital
133 Sukhumvit 49, Klongtan Nua, Vadhana, Bangkok 10110, Thailand
Tel: +66 2 711 8000
www.samitivejhospitals.com

Rutnin Eye Hospital
80/1 Sukhumvit 21 (Soi Asoke), Bangkok 10110, Thailand
Tel: +66 2 639 3399
www.rutnin.com

Singapore

Singapore has the most highly ranked health care in Asia (and is ranked sixth in the world), so it's no wonder that expats often choose to go there for medical treatment. While the care is probably better than in Thailand, it's also more expensive. Most popular is Raffles Hospital, which caters specifically to international visitors coming to Singapore for medical tourism. Raffles offers a full range of services for expats, including airport transfers, travel planning, and help with getting a GST refund for your care. General check-ups start at $120 and include blood, urine, and stool testing, while luxury check-up packages go as high as $7,000.

Singapore General Hospital is the main public hospital in town. For foreigners the prices are comparable to those at

Raffles, but if you need to stay overnight, the room rates are significantly less.

Raffles Hospital
585 North Bridge Road, Singapore 188770
Tel: +65 6311 2233
rafflesmedicalgroup.com.sg

Singapore General Hospital
Outram Road, Singapore 169608
Tel: +65 6222 3322
www.sgh.com.sg

Safety and security

The Kingdom isn't dangerous, as long as you follow sensible precautions and stay alert.

Most expats agree that Cambodia is a safe place to live. In fact, many would say that it's safer than the big cities back home. Yet while that might be true, it's still essential to be cautious and watch out for your belongings. Most victims of crimes in Cambodia don't bother to report them — filing a police report requires a payment and rarely results in the return of your possessions — so there are no good stats on how many bag-snatchings and break-ins are actually occurring. However, it's well known that there is more crime in the lead-up to major holidays such as Water Festival and Khmer New Year.

Most of the violence in the country occurs between locals, but expats are often targeted for muggings and break-ins. We've got some emergency numbers and tips for dealing with the police if you're the victim of a crime.

Robberies and bag-snatchings

The most common types of robberies in Cambodia are pickpocketings (particularly in local markets), snatch-and-grab robberies, and muggings.

In crowded local markets and particularly during festivals, men should carry their wallets in their front pockets and women should be aware of their bags at all times. Women should consider wearing their purses across the chest in order to make them more difficult to grab.

The most common type of robbery is a snatch-and-grab attack, where a man on a moto (either driver or passenger) grabs a phone, purse, bag, or camera out of your hands as he drives past. Foreigners in tuk tuks, on motos, and on foot have been targeted. When you're out and about, be very careful about using your phone, especially if it's an expensive model. Make sure you're paying attention to your surroundings and keep a firm grip on your possessions. When in a tuk tuk, hold your bag firmly to your chest or, even better, sit on it or keep it under your feet.

Be realistic and don't carry things you really can't afford to lose. If you can help it, try not to commute with your laptop. Don't play with an iPad in the back of a tuk tuk. When you are taking photos, try and stay a few feet back from the road and keep the strap around your wrist. If you need to carry your passport, make a copy and carry that instead.

During "robbery season" — the few weeks before both Khmer New Year and Water Festival — it's best for women not to carry a purse or walk around late at night. Purses draw thieves like flies to honey, and it's safer not to carry one. It's also safer to take a car taxi after dark, particularly during those weeks. In general, walking around late at night is not a great idea for women, who tend to be especially targeted for robberies.

The easiest way to prevent these kind of robberies is to be aware. If you notice a moto driving in your tuk tuk's blind spot, look directly at them. Thieves prey on inattentive expats, so staying alert can spare you becoming the victim of this type of crime.

The other common type of robbery is mugging. Unlike bag snatchings, mugging involves face-to-face contact with the perpetrators, most of whom are young men, often — surprisingly — from relatively wealthy families. Women are most often targets of these attacks, which are usually perpetrated by groups of young men, although men and couples have also been victims. This type of robbery is much more confrontational, and resisting is generally a bad idea. Violence can escalate unreasonably quickly—two Western women have been shot in Phnom Penh trying to hold on to their purses.

Hotel and apartment break-ins

Another common type of crime, primarily in Phnom Penh, is apartment and hotel break-ins. They are usually committed while the resident is out, although there have been cases of foreigners being robbed while asleep or in the other room. Most often the break-ins do not involve force; thieves come in through open windows, or use open windows to unlock the door. These sort of robberies are easy to prevent.

- Don't leave expensive items close to your windows, even if the windows have bars over them. Thieves commonly use sticks and hooks to reach in and grab phones, wallets, and other small valuables.

- Make sure your door cannot be opened via your window. This is a common problem in hotels; when windows are too close to the door, a thief can slide open the window, then reach in and unlock the door.

- Do not leave your balconies, doors, or windows open when you are in another room, unless you have bars over them.

- Don't rub your wealth in your neighbors' faces. Remember that every time you invite a tuk tuk driver inside, there is the chance he will tell everyone on your block exactly what he saw. Leaving cash and electronics sitting around will lead locals to think you're extremely wealthy and worthy of a break-in.

LIVING

- Bring locks from back home. Most apartments in Cambodia include at least one padlock, and sometimes several. Bringing one from home will assure you of the quality of your lock. Many of the big brand locks sold in Cambodia, such as Solex, are fakes that can be easily pried open with a screwdriver. Better be safe than sorry and bring a real one from home.

Remember that being on the third or fourth floor does not protect you. Many apartment break-ins are on high floors and are presumably carried out by neighbors.

Emergency numbers and dealing with the police

In Cambodia, police are some of the lowest paid workers in the country, making so little that it's impossible to support a family on salary alone. Therefore, they supplement their income by requiring fees for services rendered. What this means is that if you are the victim of a crime, you should expect to pay a small bribe to the police in order to report your crime and get a police report written. (If you have travel insurance, you'll need a police report to file a claim.) When dealing with the police, remain calm and collected. Start your offer at $5. Depending on the value of the items you've lost and how hysterical you act, you can end up paying substantially more, though most expats report paying $20 or less.

In most of Cambodia the police speak very little English, so it's best to bring a translator with you, be it a friend, hotel employee, or tuk tuk driver. If it's either of the latter, expect to tip them, too. In Siem Reap there are active tourist police who are supposed to speak English (Tel: 012 402 424; 012 969 991; 012 838 768), while in Phnom Penh the so-called tourist police speak little to no English (Tel: 023 726 158; 097 778 0002).

If you've been the victim of a crime, report it to your embassy. They can help you replace your passport, put you in contact with local attorneys or translators, and help you seek medical advice if you've been hurt.

The following information is for Phnom Penh. If you are located elsewhere, find your local emergency numbers and save them so they're readily available in case you need them.

Fire Department (24 hour) Tel: 023 723 555

Police (24 Hour) Tel: 023 366 841; 023 720 235

Traffic Police Tel: 023 722 067

Ambulance Tel: 023 724 891

US Embassy: For emergencies during business hours call (023) 728 281; 023 728 051; 023 728 234. Outside of normal business hours call 023 728 000.

UK Embassy: Tel: 023 427124. Outside of normal business hours call 023 427 124; 023 428 153.

Australian Embassy: Tel: 023 213 470

Recreational drugs in Cambodia

Many expats find the temptation to take drugs in Cambodia irresistible, and their grim end is usually captured for posterity in the pages of the *Koh Santepheap Daily,* a Khmer newspaper that delights in publishing gory post-mortem photos, especially when a foreigner is involved.

Expats are offered drugs all over Cambodia, particularly in Phnom Penh's Riverside neighborhood. The purveyors usually start by offering "Ganja, ganja." If that doesn't seem to appeal, they try again with "Ice? Cocaine? Heroin?" While this may seem like a drug-taker's idea of heaven, it's really not.

Both expats and tourists meet untimely ends quite regularly in Cambodia, often under mysterious circumstances that involve drugs. Heroin is much cheaper in Cambodia than cocaine, so it is often used to cut cocaine or sold in its stead. So when abusers rack up a big line of what they think is cocaine, they may quickly find themselves unconscious. The unreliability of Cambodian information applies to drugs as much as to everything else. A tuk tuk driver will tell you he knows exactly where you are going and end up lost for an hour, so it's unrealistic to expect this same tuk tuk driver to know the difference between various Class A substances.

It's also important to remember that overdoses in Cambodia result in deaths more often than in the West because of the poor medical care available here.

While it's true that marijuana is semi-legal in Cambodia, the exceptions to the laws against marijuana possession apply only to Cambodians, who are allowed to grow a few plants for cooking—the herb is traditionally used in Khmer cuisine. The marijuana quality in Cambodia is quite poor compared to what's grown in the West, but it's undeniably cheap. Foreigners are rarely prosecuted for small amounts of marijuana, but expect to pay a few bribes if you do get caught.

Still, that's better than dealing with Cambodia's draconian laws regarding harder drugs. While the country may seem like a druggie free-for-all, dozens of foreigners locked up in Prey Sar prison would beg to disagree. They'd also beg you to know better than to mess with drugs in

Cambodia. The situation here is quite different than it is at home, and the fear of ending up dead or crammed into a sweaty, overcrowded cell with 30 shirtless Cambodian men should—along with Cambodia's ridiculously low alcohol prices—persuade you to stick to the bars instead.

For those who are looking for help with an alcohol or substance abuse problem, it's probably no surprise that rehabilitation options in Cambodia are sub-par. However, there are English-language meetings of Alcoholics Anonymous in Phnom Penh, Siem Reap, and Sihanoukville. Contact **Alcoholics Anonymous Cambodia** for more information (www.aacambodia.org).

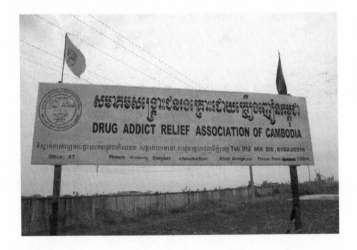

Getting help

Going to rehab in Cambodia is not recommended.

Advice for women

The experience of female expats in Cambodia is somewhat different from that of their male peers — better in many ways, but sometimes more challenging.

On the one hand, Western women — or at least young, good-looking ones — have clear advantages over their male counterparts when it comes to getting teaching jobs and free drinks. They're also almost entirely immune to the type of street harassment they may have experienced in the West. At the same time, things that women take for granted at home, such as being able to buy their familiar brand of birth control, may not be so easy in Cambodia. The situation in that regard is rapidly improving, however. With each passing month Cambodia grows more cosmopolitan, particularly in Phnom Penh and Siem Reap. And the little things that used to be so difficult — such as trying to find a store that sells tampons — are becoming only a memory, at least in the cities.

Not that everything is perfect, but foreign women won't generally find Cambodia a difficult place to live.

For more advice for women, see the Women's health chapter in the Health and medical care section, page 120.

Clothing and dress

One of the great joys of being an expat female in Cambodia is that Cambodian men are quite polite and reticent about harassing foreign women. For many expats, the almost complete absence of street harassment is one of the most refreshing things about the place. However, foreign women who walk around in clothes that are very revealing by Cambodian standards will often find themselves on the receiving end of unwanted male attention or, at the very least, looks of disdain from Cambodian women.

Cambodian women dress quite conservatively, keeping their shoulders and knees covered. Most women wear long-sleeved shirts and long pants or a long skirt (and even more often, matching long-sleeved cotton pajama sets). Although some of the younger generation are starting to dress less conservatively, keep in mind that a large percentage of the

LIVING

Beautiful bride

Weddings are a most important day for Khmer women.

population believes that a woman wearing short shorts and a tank top is probably a sex worker. Expats of Asian background will find that they are held to a higher standard than other foreigners, possibly because locals assume they are Khmer.

During the day, it's best to not show too much skin if you can help it. That said, many choose to bare a lot of flesh, and it's not uncommon to see backpackers outside the Royal Palace wearing very little. At night the rules loosen up a bit, because all of the nice Khmer girls are in bed by 10 p.m. At nightclubs in Phnom Penh you'll see expats and Cambodians alike dressed to kill and showing a little leg in the process.

When visiting pagodas (*wats*) and temples (including Angkor Wat), it is considered disrespectful to be uncovered. In that setting, exposing your knees and shoulders is not polite. While it's rare that you'll be refused entrance or called out on your bad behavior, that does not mean that Cambodians don't mind or don't take offense. Yes, it may be hot out there, but that's no excuse for disrespecting the local sacred religious spots. Women and men should wear long sleeves and long pants or skirts that cover the knees for these occasions.

Women and safety

We've covered most of the key issues in the **Safety and security** section (page 137), but it's important to remember that women—both Khmer and foreign—are often the targets of street crime, and their purses and jewelry are most often what's taken. It's best not to wear expensive-looking jewelry when on the street and on motos. Khmer women who wear gold necklaces often have them yanked off while stopped in traffic.

Women should also be very careful with their purses while riding in tuk tuks or on motos. Hold your bag tightly to your chest, or better yet, sit on it or keep it under your feet. Playing with expensive phones while traveling or on the street is also not a great idea; a common theft involves two men on a moto driving by and swiping the phone out of the hands of someone on the street or on the back of a moto.

While walking, wear your purse across your chest. At night, do not walk alone — it's sad but true that you are less likely to be the victim of a robbery if you have a male companion. Thieves seem to particularly target women walking solo and in pairs.

Women should take extra precautions when out at nightclubs or late-night bars. As everywhere, don't leave your drink unattended. When heading home late at night always take a car taxi, or tuk tuk that you trust, and ask your driver to walk you to your door. Many robberies happen outside homes while the residents fumble with their keys.

It should be noted that while women are often the targets of petty crimes and theft, sexual harassment of foreign women is quite rare in Cambodia. Expat women are happy to find out that the sort of low-level street harassment of women that is common in so many places is virtually non-existent in Cambodia. Foreign women are also rarely the targets of sexual assaults. Unfortunately, Khmer women are not so lucky. Sexual assaults happen regularly in the Kingdom, but locals are almost always the victims.

LIVING

1-2-3 lift

Running the bamboo
train is a lot of work!

Motivation on the go

Fortunately, making a living in Cambodia isn't
too difficult.

Part Four

Working in Cambodia

While many move to Cambodia in order to retire or pursue artistic endeavors, others come to pursue employment opportunities in the Kingdom of Wonder.

We'll tell you all about employment in Cambodia, from how to find a job to how to start a business. Whether you're working for someone else or for yourself, it's important to know how Cambodian culture affects the way business is done here. If you're running a business, there's even more to learn. And of course we've covered work permits and income taxes.

We've got a special section for those who are interested in teaching English, including how to find an English-teaching job in Cambodia.

WORKING

Employment in Cambodia

Whether you want to start a business, work with an NGO, or get a job in the private sector, employment opportunities abound in Cambodia.

Pay in Cambodia ranges from Western-scale wages to bartending gigs where you might get a couple bucks a night plus free drinks. Many expats come to Cambodia to volunteer or intern for a small stipend and get international development experience. While the number of private-sector and English-teaching jobs available to expats is quite large, most do not command a huge salary. Still, they offer enough to allow you to live an easy life in an inexpensive country. Those who work for NGOs (nonprofit Non-Governmental Organizations) experience a greater range of salary, from the lowly volunteers to the well-paid country managers.

Another perk of working in Cambodia is the huge number of public holidays — there are 27 scheduled for 2013. Most expats will also get some regular vacation days as well. And one of the things that expats most appreciate about Cambodia, in addition to the country's lax approach to visas, is its laissez-faire attitude toward work permits. Although technically work permits are required, in practice they are not needed for many jobs. If a permit is necessary, your employer should obtain one for you through the Ministry of the Interior.

Many expats who move to Cambodia choose to teach English. Teaching jobs are plentiful and, while most are low-paid, there are some plum posts at the genuine international schools for those with actual teaching qualifications. **For those without such qualifications, never fear — there are jobs available to you, too.**

Other expats choose to set up a business in Cambodia, whether a "lifestyle" business that aims only to break even or an ambitious enterprise that will build you a fortune in the Kingdom of Wonder.

Work permits

It's important to note that work permits and visas are not the same thing. In theory, although you may have gotten a year-long visa (often called a business visa), that doesn't necessarily give you the right to work in Cambodia. In practice, Cambodia is one of the least regulated countries in the world when it comes to visas and employment, and many expats do not have the work permits that they ostensibly require.

There are two types of work permits in Cambodia: temporary and permanent. Temporary work permits are for most regular expats and last the length of the individual's visa. Permanent work permits are reserved for major investors and friends of people in high places.

In order to get a work permit, your employer needs to apply for you through the Ministry of Interior. Essentially, this is entirely up to your employer, but if they do want you to have a work permit, you will have to provide the following:

- 3 sets of Application Form as issued by the Ministry of Interior

- Passport with valid visa

- 3 photographs (4×6), taken from the front without hat or glasses

WORKING

- Certificate of Health from a physician in Cambodia

- Written work contract

- Insurance policy issued by employer or any insurance company

You will also have to pay a fee. Although the actual amount of the fee is not stated in Prakas 555, the document concerning Cambodia's "Management of Foreigners' Work Permits," it's generally known to be $100.

At the current time, work permits are essentially a non-issue. You do not, in practice, need a work permit to get hired at a company in Cambodia. Most expats do not have them and the government rarely asks about it. There have been more crackdowns recently—they usually last a few days and a few people are told they need to procure permits—but then everything goes back to business as usual.

Most English schools, for example, have a small percentage of teachers with work permits that can be shown to the police when they come by to ask. The schools don't bother to obtain permits for the rest of the staff. Although this is the case at the time of writing, it is likely that at some point in the future laws about work permits for expats will be more vigorously enforced.

For those who are required to get one, a work permit usually costs $100 per year. However, be aware that in recent crackdowns foreigners have been required to pay $100 per year backdated for the entire time they've spent in Cambodia, not just the current year.

Finding work

For those looking to work in the private sector or at an NGO, there are a few things to keep in mind. (Prospective English teachers, we've got tips for you as well later in the chapter.)

Finding a job once you are already on the ground in Cambodia is much easier than securing one before you arrive. Many companies won't respond to CVs from outside of the country. On the other hand, if you're looking for the sort of high-paying job that comes complete with a sweet expat package, know that salary offers are often lower for in-country candidates than for those applying from outside of the country. Either way, finding work in Cambodia isn't too hard to do, especially if you're willing to be flexible.

Popular job listing sites like **CamHR** (camhr.com) and **Bong Thom Classifieds** (www.bongthom.com) are a good place to start. The English-language newspapers also have job listings; they are a particularly good place to find NGO jobs. The **Phnom Penh Post** has a print and online version (www.phnompenhpost.com) with job listings, while the *Cambodia Daily* is print only.

There are also a few headhunter firms working in Cambodia, namely **Top Recruitment** (www.top-recruitment.com) and **HR Inc.** (www.hrinc.com.kh). If you're looking for a job in the private sector, these are a good bet. They also offer many NGO and development opportunities and are a good place to look for consulting gigs.

For those looking in the NGO and development sectors, **Reliefweb Cambodia** (reliefweb.int/country/khm) has job postings by the various development organizations and the United Nations. You can find additional UN jobs in the procurement section of specific UN websites. **Idealist** (www.idealist.org) also offers many job listings and internships in Cambodia.

WORKING

The easiest way to find jobs in Cambodia, though, is through other expats. While the expat community is growing larger every day, it's still small enough that finding a job the old-fashioned way—through someone you know—isn't too hard. There are many opportunities for networking, particularly in Phnom Penh. Many of the networking events in the capital can also lead to employment in other parts of the country.

The **American Cambodia Business Council** (www. amchamcambodia.net), known as AmCham, "serves as the voice of American business within the Cambodian private sector" and regularly holds networking events and other activities, sometimes cosponsored with the **British Chamber of Commerce Cambodia** (www.bbacambodia.com). The British Chamber also holds its own regular networking events and is a good business resource for expats of all nationalities, not just Brits.

Drinks by Design (www.facebook.com/pages/Drinks-By-Design/256108197769622) holds informational sessions and networking events for design professionals and, occasionally, for a broader audience of creative types. On the last Wednesday of every month the Intercontinental Hotel in Phnom Penh holds a wine-and-cheese night that is an informal expat networking event, where it's nearly impossible *not* to meet some of the private-sector business people in town.

PERSPECTIVE

My background is in the publishing industry, so whenever moving to a foreign country, I research the leading English publications. In Cambodia a friend of mine knew the publisher of a great regional publication and put me in touch. I have been working here for almost two years now.

Daisy Walsh
media sales executive

I volunteered with an AusAID program for 18 months before I got my paid job in Cambodia. I think that volunteering is a great way to get into the development industry.

Anna Olsen
technical officer

I saw the position advertised on either BongThom or ReliefWeb and had heard through friends that it was a good place to work. I applied, interviewed three times and did a written test, and then got the job.

Luke Gracie
NGO program manager

I began by doing freelance graphic design work for local companies — logos, brochures, copywriting, etc. As the internet started to take hold in Cambodia, I started to do a little bit of that, too. One client led to two, then three, and before long I had a small base of clients. I think longevity has been a large part of my success, in that I have been here a while, I know a few people, and I work hard — nights, evenings, weekends — whatever it takes to get the job done.

Robert Starkweather
web developer
www.k4media.com

WORKING

Doing business in Cambodia

Working in Cambodia provides an excellent opportunity for cultural immersion, whether you work for an established business or start your own.

Although it's true that Cambodians do not expect foreigners to behave the way they do, it's important to know how Cambodian culture plays into the workplace environment.

Cambodian society is highly hierarchical. For example, in meetings staff will probably not be eager to volunteer great ideas. Rather, they are more likely to agree with whatever the boss suggests, even if they know it's not in the best interest of the company. As a foreigner working in a Cambodian company, you may be seen as slightly outside of these rules, but it's still best to try and be as diplomatic as possible.

Understanding the concept of face is key. (Read more about face in the **Get to know Khmer culture** section, page 6.) Face is honor, reputation, dignity, and social importance all rolled into one. An employee will lose face if ever taken to task or told that he is doing something incorrectly in front of his peers. Any sort of negative feedback should be delivered privately, in a calm manner and as indirectly as you can stand. Giving suggestions for improvement rather than criticism is also a good way to proceed.

Face will affect you at work in many subtle ways. Your colleagues will always say they understand you, even when they don't. When pressed, they will make up answers to questions you pose, in order to not admit that they do not know the answer. When you ask them to do something they disagree with, they will answer "Yes, yes," and then not do it, much to your annoyance. In these cases, their intention is not to defy you, but rather to save face for both of you by avoiding an open confrontation.

You'll find that your colleagues will also try and help you save face by not telling you about any mistakes you might be making, however helpful that information might be to you. You may discover people doing what seem like ridiculous workarounds for extended periods of time to protect you or their colleagues from realizing that you or they are doing something incorrectly and make sure that no one loses face.

Exhibiting anger or losing your temper is seen as a major loss of face, not only for yourself but for those around you. Remaining calm and learning deep-breathing techniques will help immensely in these situations or, when that fails, a stiff drink.

Yet for all their concern with saving face, Cambodians will often treat their foreign peers in ways that would be considered unabashedly rude in the West. Be prepared to be told how fat you are by your Cambodian colleagues on a regular basis. Some will go so far as to pinch your belly to make their point. Cambodians love to discuss the minutiae of each other's appearance, and you will be included in this interaction. Unfortunately, Cambodians do not seem to realize that telling foreigners that they are sweaty/pudgy/freckled would be considered a face-losing insult in the foreigners' home countries.

Cambodians also feel comfortable publicly making negative comments about other issues that Westerners regard as out of bounds in the workplace, such as your marital status, sexual orientation, or income. Your choice is to either grin and bear it or politely tell them—in private—that you'd prefer not to hear how ugly/tall/single you are every day.

WORKING

INTERVIEW WITH AN EXPAT

What's the most important thing you've learned about doing business in Cambodia?

Not to expect things to run on your timetable. Not staff, not customers, not suppliers, not meetings. If you do not learn to be more flexible in this regard, you can drive yourself insane.

What are the best things about working in Cambodia?

The scope of opportunity here, the chance to work with, or for, companies that you may not even get an interview with back home. Or, if you're setting up your own business, you can have a 100 percent foreign-owned company here. The government is very pro-business and is actually very approachable. Work here is (usually) a lot less stressful than roles I have had in London, New York, Milan, Paris, etc. Business visa requirements are just: turn up, pay the fee, forget about it for the next twelve months and then repeat.

What are the biggest challenges of working in Cambodia?

If during the course of running a business, or even just working here, you have to manage multiple members of local staff, you need to understand that in Cambodian culture, work

Starting a business

Out of 183 economies, the World Bank has ranked Cambodia 171st in terms of ease of setting up a new business. Cambodia saddles would-be entrepreneurs with a plethora of procedures to follow, and the average number of days it takes to register a business clocks in at 85—much more than in neighboring countries. Registering a business in Cambodia is complicated and expensive, and if you're from one of the growing number of countries that prohibit their citizens from paying bribes abroad—and in fact will prosecute them for doing so—you're looking at some tough choices.

comes in a distant third in their priorities. Family comes first, then second are their friends or social network. Then work follows. What this means is that if there is a problem in the family, quite often people just do not come to work, do not call and tell you, and upon their return they often use the phrase (in English) 'Too busy to come to work.' You can try and put safeguards in place to offset this, as well as explain why you should at least get a phone call explaining that they will not be in today. But that takes time and is not always understood, as from their perspective you are the one acting oddly, and not them.

The local educational institutions provide a low quality of training and education. This results in a workforce that needs extensive training when they enter the job market. Their capacity needs to be built almost from scratch.

The 23-plus days of public holidays make running a business difficult at certain times of the year. It also reduces Cambodia's competitive advantage over such countries as China and India — and, in the near future, Burma.

Darren Conquest
chairman, British Chamber of
Commerce Cambodia
www.bbacambodia.com

A fair amount of palm-greasing, or "tea money," is required to start a business. Each step of the process requires fees, many of which are not strictly legal. For example, once your company is fully registered, in order to stay compliant with Cambodian law you must pay your taxes. In order to pay your taxes, you need to pay an unofficial $20 "facilitation fee" at the tax office each month. If you don't, your taxes won't get registered as being paid. There are no easy answers, but be assured that slowly but surely things are getting better. Despite all of this, the Cambodian government is very pro-business, and allows 100-percent foreign-owned companies, unlike some of their neighbors.

WORKING

Many businesses fly under the radar of the authorities, and others choose to take over from existing businesses that have already completed the required paperwork. If you do decide to start your own business, it's worth it to hire a local fixer to guide you through the process. This will usually cost around $500 for a small business and will save you a lot of time and headaches.

If you're looking for more information on running a business in Cambodia, contact the **American Cambodia Business Council** (www.amchamcambodia.net) or the **British Chamber of Commerce Cambodia** (www.bbacambodia.com).

Also, the World Bank's **Doing Business in Cambodia** site has a lot of valuable information (www.doingbusiness.org/data/exploreeconomies/cambodia/).

BNG Legal has an easy-to-understand guide, *Maintaining Corporate Compliance in Cambodia,* that's a good read for those wanting to do things properly (https://www.bnglegal.com/uploads/reports/Cambodian%20Corporate%20Compliance.pdf).

Running a business

Things are different here, so the more you know about Cambodian culture and mores, the easier a time you'll have getting your business up and running.

If you're starting your own business, it pays to learn a little bit about the religious customs of the country. When starting a new endeavour (opening a new office, say), Cambodians ask Buddhist monks to come bless the project, offering them food and a small stipend for their trouble. Additionally, businesses should have a spirit house out front or inside. Generally these are attended to by the cleaning staff, who make sure that they are properly stocked with offerings. If you want your employees to be happy, it's best to

PERSPECTIVE

It seems that many people come to Cambodia with preconceived ideas, and a lot of times those ideas do not match the realities of this quickly changing market. If you plan to work here or start a business, take your time, get to know the country and the market, and be ready to adjust your plans accordingly.

Bryse Gaboury
co-founder,
Advancing Engineering

Be patient. Do not try and set up your new business in one day. **Do your business research and market research first. Make contact with as many expat business people as possible to get a better understanding of the business environment here. Network and go to the many business networking events. The British Chamber of Commerce is one of the most active in Cambodia and accepts guests and associate members of all nationalities.**

Darren Conquest
chairman, British Chamber of Commerce Cambodia
www.bbacambodia.com

conduct these rituals, lest everything that goes wrong in the office be blamed on your failure to comply with local beliefs.

Additionally, learning Khmer is important if you want to be able to effectively communicate with your staff.

The educational system in Cambodia does not promote critical thinking, so it's usually best to give very clear, specific instructions to your employees about what you are looking for from them. Even when tasks seem quite simple, it's important to go over them again and again, and then to do refresher trainings every few months.

As the boss, it's important to project an authoritative image. Dressing well and driving an expensive car go a long way to establishing respect among the locals. Conversely, if you dress too casually, it will be much harder to earn their respect. With your employees, make sure you remain open

WORKING

and friendly, give bonuses and time off for Khmer New Year, and accept the occasional obvious lie when an employee does not make it to work, lest you be seen as mean or cheap. To some degree bosses are expected to be benefactors toward their staff, and so it's important to have occasional staff parties or meals where you pick up the bill.

Asking your employees to work hard is seen as quite mean; be prepared to hire three or four people to do a job that two could easily do. Cambodians generally have a laid-back attitude about work, and when you review their salaries, you'll understand why.

Cambodian employees can be difficult to understand if you don't bother to learn a bit about Cambodian culture, but they have plenty of positive qualities. Many Cambodians are happy to take a low-paying job and stay in it for years. If their bosses treat them kindly they will be quite loyal. In addition, Cambodian employees are more likely to work cooperatively.

When you move up the pay scale and start hiring Cambodians who have been educated abroad, many of the negative qualities discussed here do not hold true. Members of the younger generation are better educated and far more ambitious than their elders, and more willing to put time and energy into building their careers.

Another issue that expats face when running a business in Cambodia is being asked to pay extra, unofficial fees for services from private companies and government officials. These fees are occasionally semi-official, such as CINTRI charging foreigners more for garbage disposal. And unofficial charges, which some might call bribes, are requested as the price of accomplishing just about anything having to do with the government. As a business person, you will have to decide which of these fees you are willing to pay and which you want to fight. If you do choose to negotiate, it's usually best to have a Khmer partner with you (or in your stead) to handle the negotiations.

INTERVIEW WITH AN EXPAT

Any tips for running a business in Cambodia?

Hold fast against paying the "*barang* tax"; you can usually prevail. Have a Khmer you trust fight those battles on your behalf. It would seem obvious, but know your market. Expect to invest a lot of time and effort in staff training. Stay on the right side of officialdom. One must accept the culture of corruption to some extent, but keeping things friendly is not expensive.

Bar owner, Phnom Penh

What about tips for dealing with bureaucracy in Cambodia?

Get a Khmer to do it! Whenever I have had to deal with an RGC [Royal Government of Cambodia] ministry or department, when I knew in advance that some 'facilitation' would be required, I would not attend the meeting personally. I would usually designate a senior staff member (often the finance director) to go and resolve the situation.

Businessman, Phnom Penh

WORKING

Street scene

Small businesses are everywhere in Cambodia

Teaching English

Jobs teaching English in Cambodia are plentiful and easy to find.

There are many, many expats in Cambodia teaching English, from qualified professionals with Western teaching degrees and years of experience to backpackers volunteering for a few weeks at questionable orphanages. While many expats are genuinely here to teach, it must be said that teaching professionals can make more money in neighboring countries in Asia. The average salary for foreign English teachers in Phnom Penh hovers around $10 to $14 per hour. The rate is slightly less in Siem Reap and less still in Sihanoukville.

The majority of expats choose to teach in Cambodia because the barriers to entry are quite low. Getting a job without any sort of degree is not difficult, particularly if one is light-skinned and not unpleasant looking. If one is wildly unattractive, it's best to have a bachelor's degree, but no specific teaching degree is required. In general, it's easier to get a job in Cambodia if you are young, white, and female, but those who are none of the above can find work as well; it's just not as ridiculously easy.

Having a TEFL (Teaching English as a Foreign Language) certificate or CELTA (Certificate in English Language Teaching to Adults) will increase your odds of getting a higher-paying job at a better school. If you want to work at one of the genuine international schools in town, you'll need a real teaching degree and previous teaching experience. The difference in pay between the regular English schools and the international schools is significant.

INTERVIEW WITH AN EXPAT

Why did you start teaching English in Cambodia?

I'm working on an **MA-ESL** [master's degree in English as a Second Language] and I chose to teach in Cambodia because, basically, anybody can just fly into the country, pay for a business visa, and start applying for jobs. No questions asked! No approval process, no sponsor required, no hassles.

What's the best part about teaching English in Cambodia?

I'm currently in a situation where I teach at a good school, and I take the job seriously. I make a sincere effort to provide my students with a good education, and I get a lot of satisfaction and fulfillment out of it. And I only need to work part-time in order to make a living and support myself here in Cambodia. I don't live extravagantly, but I get by all right, and I have plenty of free time to enjoy myself.

What's the most difficult part about teaching English in Cambodia?

There are a lot of good (or potentially good) teachers whose talents are being wasted by toiling away for schools that are a complete joke. There are no educational standards and the administrators at many of the schools are corrupt. They take bribes or allow students to cheat in order to retain their tuition. It can all be quite disheartening if you are working in an environment like that.

Ned Kelly
English teacher

WORKING

The thing to remember is that many Cambodians put aside all of their extra earnings to save up for English courses. Being an English teacher who is grossly unqualified to teach is truly unfair to these students. While many schools think that being a native English speaker is qualification enough for a job, if you want to be a good teacher it's worth getting a TEFL certification, or better yet, a CELTA, from an accredited institution. If you don't have either of these, consider trying to get some ESL teaching experience at home before you come. Or try volunteering as an English teacher for a few months in Cambodia when you first arrive. Many women and children's organizations are eager to find volunteer teachers who are willing to stay more than the week or two that most backpackers offer. Westerners often find that after a few weeks of volunteering they either take to teaching like a duck to water, or realize that it's not the career path for them. Better to find out where you stand before you sign a contract and commit to a full term.

Depending on your school, teaching in Cambodia can be an exercise in frustration or incredibly rewarding. This is why many teachers switch schools regularly, especially at first. Classrooms can be raucous places, filled with children who have never experienced discipline in their lives and are more eager to show up the teacher than to conjugate English verbs. On the other hand, many students are bright and eager to learn and develop great relationships with their teachers.

It's also important to remember that most teachers are paid only for their classroom hours and not preparation time. Note that the pay for teachers is generally taxed at around 15 percent.

Finding work as an English teacher

While many prospective expats work themselves into a lather trying to find work before they arrive in Cambodia, old hands know that the best thing to do is just show up.

It's true that if you want to work at the international schools, applying in advance from outside of the country seems to help. These schools (such as ISPP and Northbridge) require real teaching degrees and previous experience. They often (but not always) offer higher salaries and airfare to those who apply from outside of the country.

For everyone else, especially those who are utterly unqualified, don't bother applying before you arrive. Most jobs are not posted online, and when they are it's rare that anyone will actually read and respond to your email inquiry. If they do, they will expect you to be available for an interview immediately.

Once you are in the country, make up a clean, simple CV and, if you don't have facial tattoos, attach a headshot of yourself in a suit. (It's standard protocol for Cambodians to submit photos with their job applications.) You can get passport-sized photos made at any photography shop for a few thousand riel.

After you've got your CV and headshot ready, get out and pound the pavement. The days of dreadlocked backpackers in Beer Lao tank tops getting hired off the street to teach English are almost over, and while it's possible to get a job looking like a complete mess, you'll find that your presentation often directly correlates to the salary you are offered and the type of school that is willing to consider you. So get a haircut, put on a shirt with a collar (if you're a guy, add a tie and shave to the equation), and hit the street.

The best plan is just to go door to door to English schools, smiling and handing out CVs. Most expats are able to get at least one job offer after spending a day or two looking. If you have a CELTA, A.C.E. is one of the highest-paying (and only internationally-accredited) English schools. For others, Home of English, Pannasastra University, and ELT are often hiring.

Be warned, though, that most English schools will only offer you minimal and unappealing hours (early mornings or weekends) your first term. After that, you can negotiate more teaching hours, preferably at more convenient times.

WORKING

Taxes

Here's the low-down on Cambodia's tax limbo, which can be confusing to say the least.

One of the major causes of corruption in Cambodia is reputed to be the government's inability to legally bring in revenue, in part because almost no one in the country pays taxes.

That's not to say there aren't laws on the books demanding that everyone pay taxes. There are. But in practice a large percentage of Cambodians and expats alike do not pay taxes on their incomes.

For tax purposes, people are considered residents of Cambodia if they have a principal place of abode in Cambodia or are present more than 182 days in the country in any 12-month period ending in the current tax year. Residents are liable for taxes on worldwide income and profits, while non-residents are only taxed on Cambodia-sourced income. Residents are taxed on salary at rates of:

- 10 percent for those making between $312.50 and $2,150 per month

- 15 percent for those making between $2,150 and $3,12

- 20 percent for those making $3,120 or more each month

- Non-residents get taxed a flat 20 percent.

- For income from personal services, the tax rate is 15 percent.

- For other, non-salary income the tax rate is usually 20 percent, but higher for certain things such as mineral exploitation.

The obligation to withhold and pay tax rests with the employer, and many employers choose not to do so. This leaves their employees in a sort of legal limbo. At the time of writing, there is no easy way for individuals to report and pay taxes, and it must be said that most choose not to do so. It seems likely that this will change in the future, but at the current time there is little enforcement against individuals who do not comply with Cambodian tax law.

PricewaterhouseCoopers has a good, free guide to taxes in Cambodia (www.pwc.com/en_KH/kh/publications/2012/assets/cambodia-tax-book2012-05042012.pdf).

BNG Legal also offers an easy-to-understand tax guide for individuals in Cambodia (www.bnglegal.com/uploads/reports/Individual%20Income%20Tax.pdf).

Tax writeoff

Worry about your tan, not your taxes.

Volunteering in Cambodia

Everything you ever wanted to know (and a few things you didn't) about volunteering in Cambodia!

Every year thousands of well-intentioned foreigners come to Cambodia to volunteer. A few days of volunteer work have become as *de rigueur* for visitors to Cambodia as visiting the temples of Angkor. As a result, volunteering has become a full-fledged industry here and, lately, the subject of a lot of negative press.

Most volunteers choose to work with Cambodian children, usually by teaching English in orphanages. Be aware, though, that these Cambodian orphanages exist only to cater to foreign tourists. In fact, the vast majority of children who are placed in orphanages in Cambodia are not orphans and have at least one living parent. But demand from foreign tourists to visit Cambodian orphanages and work with Cambodian children is so high that parents are often offered powerful financial incentives to place their children in these so-called orphanages, or are promised that they will be provided with a great education, which is often not the case.

Yes, this means just what you think it does: Cambodian kids are being taken out of their homes in order to give foreigners the chance to post photos of themselves hanging out with Cambodian orphans on Facebook. Children are being kept out of school so that they can instead learn to dance and put on orphan dance performances on the streets of Siem Reap. Pretty grim, eh?

Understandably, all those Western volunteers would like to believe that they are different, that the work they are doing does not harm Cambodian children. Unfortunately, they're wrong. If you want to work with children in Cambodia, first ask yourself if you are qualified to work with children at home. Most Westerners would be horrified at the idea of dozens of Cambodians flooding their child's classroom each year—especially if said Cambodians had no qualifications to teach, had no teaching experience, underwent no background checks, and proceeded to post photos of the children all over Facebook. If you can't imagine a school in your home country allowing that, I'm sure you can understand why many feel that it's not appropriate for Cambodian children, either.

Unless you have a very specific skill set, there is almost no volunteer work in Cambodia that you can effectively do if you're here less than three months. Most reputable organizations no longer accept volunteers who are not willing to stay for at least 3 or 6 or sometimes 12 months. Think about it: students don't learn English when their teachers are coming in and out for two-week stints. They learn the same things—like the alphabet and how to count to ten—over and over again, but never get a deeper understanding of the language. Imagine if your whole childhood education had been in the hands of short-term substitute teachers. Many of the schools and "orphanages" that use volunteers do so to avoid having to pay for permanent teachers. More generally, organizations that welcome short-term volunteers are all too often in it only for the money.

Which brings us to the money. Many organizations that charge you to volunteer with children are highly suspect and often do not have the best interests of the children in mind. Organizations that do not require background checks most definitely do not have the best interests of children in mind.

Most work that you can do in Cambodia could be done as well or better by a Cambodian. Building houses and teaching may be eye-opening experiences for the volunteers,

WORKING

but there is no shortage of Cambodian workers and these volunteer positions can take badly needed jobs away from Cambodians.

By now it's becoming widely recognized that short-term volunteering is not an effective solution to Cambodia's problems and in fact may do more harm than good. However, there are many long-term volunteering programs that are highly regarded.

- For Americans, check out the Peace Corps (www.peacecorps.gov).

- For Australians, there is the AYAD program (www.ayad.com.au) and AusAid's VIDA program (www.volunteering.austraining.com.au).

- For the British, there's the VSO program (www.vso.org.uk).

If you're still intent on visiting for the short term, check out **PEPY Tours** (www.pepytours.com). They offer educational bicycle trips and other tours that help visitors learn about the complexity of development work.

If you'd like to learn more about responsible volunteering and tourism in Cambodia, Friends International, Cambodia's leading child-safety organization, has plenty of information on the topic on their **When Children Become Tourist Attractions** site (www.thinkchildsafe.org/thinkbeforevisiting).

Daniela Papi, founder of PEPY, an educational development NGO, has written extensively about voluntourism in Cambodia on her blog, **Lessons I Learned** (lessonsilearned.org). **Learning Service: Tips for Learning Before Helping** (lessonsilearned.org/2012/07/learning-service-guidelines) is a good place to start for those considering volunteering. She's also written a great article about volunteering in Cambodia that wanna-be volunteers would do well to read, **"Voluntourism: What can go wrong when trying to do right?"** (www.huffingtonpost.com/daniela-papi/voluntourism_b_1525532.html).

WORKING

Classroom antics

A huge percentage of the population in Cambodia are eager to learn English.

INTERVIEW WITH AN EXPAT

Is there any way for people to volunteer responsibly in Cambodia?

Travelers looking to "help" in Cambodia, or anywhere they don't know well, should remember the most important lessons I learned during six years in Cambodia: We have to learn before we can help. If we skip over the learning part and are driven by our sympathy, we can often cause more harm than good: working for a corrupt organization, investing time and energy in efforts that perpetuate rather than counter poverty, etc. If we want to lead with empathy, rather than sympathy, we need to be able to put ourselves in someone else's shoes. And in order to do that, we have to know them, their culture, their history, and have a view into the long-term impacts of our work. So we should travel to learn first.

But can people volunteer responsibly? Of course! The problem is, people usually don't go abroad to volunteer with a goal of maximizing their impact. Understandably, they usually also want to have fun,

so oftentimes they want to do something active — paint something, build something, or play with kids — rather than less 'fun' work. If you are an accountant, there are probably tons of NGOs who need to understand accounting and tax law practices in your country, if it is a source of their donations. Or if you are a web or graphic designer, there are always tons of people who would want your help. The best matches will be ones where an organization has identified a need and is looking to have someone fill that role as a training position for a more full-time staff person, and where the volunteer applies to fill the role with the specific skills necessary.

How can someone figure out if the organization they want to volunteer with is a reputable one?

Once again, making the choice of where to give our time requires us to learn first. It requires us to do some work. You can't just go online and see which ones are 'great' organizations, as unfortunately in international aid the

beneficiaries themselves rarely get a chance to directly voice their feedback (and reviews from other donors or volunteers are not what you should be looking for). Ask people online, such as others you are connected to in that sector or who are working in that country, and ask the organizations themselves for feedback. Any organization that will not engage you in discussions about their own weaknesses or areas of growth, or that is willing to put you in a volunteer position that you are not qualified for, is probably not one you want to be giving your time to.

Why shouldn't I volunteer with kids? And what's wrong with volunteering at orphanages?

A recent **UNICEF** report showed that **76** percent of Cambodian 'orphans' living in orphanages have one or more living parents. Actually, the number of true orphans has gone down, but the rate of orphanage growth has risen with the growth of the tourism sector. Any orphanage that will let you in off the street for a day or a week without requiring background checks or without requiring that you are qualified for a specific role is not one at which you should be volunteering. Many orphanages in Cambodia are businesses. They will ask you to take a 'free visit to our orphanage' and then tell you tales of poverty. These institutions are separating kids who have parents from their families and communities, oftentimes for their own financial gain. I've done this kind of volunteering myself, and I've learned from watching the negative impacts of this harmful practice grow: a volunteer visit to an orphanage might be a feel-good experience for a traveler, but it is an immensely damaging practice for the families of Cambodia. Don't do it.

Daniela Papi
founder of PEPY

WORKING

Resources

For More Information

Whether you're already in Cambodia or just
looking to make the move, our list of web
resources (including travel sites, expat forums,
and job boards) and suggested reading is sure
to help.

Summer reading

If you want to learn more about Cambodia,
there's lots of information out there.

Web resources

The internet offers a wealth of information about the Kingdom of Wonder and multiple ways of learning about life here, finding work, and connecting with other expats.

Travel around Cambodia

Canby Publications
www.canbypublications.com
One of the best and most frequently-updated travel resources for Cambodia, produced entirely by Cambodia residents. They offer free guidebooks with excellent maps that can be found in hotels and restaurants in Phnom Penh, Siem Reap and Sihanoukville.

Lonely Planet's Thorn Tree: Cambodia
www.lonelyplanet.com/thorntree/forum.
    jspa?forumID=24&keywordid=92
Lonely Planet's Thorn Tree forum for Cambodia is a heavily trafficked site featuring advice (and arguments) from backpackers and other independent travelers.

Travelfish
www.travelfish.org
Offering independent reviews and loads of advice, Travelfish is a great resource for travel around Cambodia, including the lesser-known spots.

RESOURCES

Cambodia expat forums and online groups

Khmer 440 Forum

www.khmer440.com/chat_forum

The Khmer440 forum is one of the best resources for up-to-date Cambodia information and issues relating to expats. You'll find lots of long-term expats using the forum here, and they're always willing to help out a newbie. News often shows up on Khmer440 before it makes the English-language newspapers.

The Cambodia Parent Network

groups.yahoo.com/group/cambodiaparentnetwork

The Cambodia Parent Network is a Yahoo Group with more than 2,500 expats (not all of them parents). It's a great source for moving sales, buying and selling, and sourcing difficult-to-find items.

Expat Advisory

www.expat-advisory.com/forum/asia/cambodia

Expat Advisory is another active expat forum in Cambodia. The main Cambodia Expat Advisory page also has news, and user-generated event listings and business listings.

Phnom Penh

Khmer440

www.khmer440.com/k

Khmer440 has restaurant reviews, news, speculation, and humorous articles about various Cambodia-related topics. The site is rapidly expanding and adds new content regularly.

Lady Penh
ladypenh.com
Lady Penh provides weekly listings of events and happenings in Phnom Penh. A great resource if you're looking for something to do in town.

Leng Pleng Gig Guide
www.lengpleng.com
Leng Pleng Gig Guide is Phnom Penh's live music guide, with listings of live music and DJ gigs around Cambodia, although most listings are in Phnom Penh.

Kampot and Kep

Kampot & Kep Noticeboard for Expats & Locals
www.facebook.com/groups/kampotandkep
The Kampot & Kep Noticeboard for Expats & Locals Facebook group is a good place to find out what's going on in Kampot and Kep, including housing notices, events, and more.

Kampto Expatica
kampotexpatica.com/forum
Kampto Expatica is a new forum where Kampot expats can exchange information on rentals, employment, buying, and selling, plus general banter. However, it's not very active.

Siem Reap

Siem Reap Expats

www.facebook.com/groups/siemreap

The Siem Reap Expats Facebook group, which is 1,500 strong, offers events, housing notices, and an opportunity to shoot the breeze with other foreign residents of Siem Reap.

Sihanoukville

Sihanoukville Expats

www.facebook.com/groups/193984980677829

The Sihanoukville Expats Facebook group is a place for Sihanoukville-based expats to share information, event listings, buy and sell offers, and housing notices. It does not welcome travel questions.

Sihanoukville Online Forums

www.sihanoukvilleonline.com/forum

The Sihanoukville Online Forums is the place to go to ask expats and Sihanoukville business owners all of your burning questions about the town and what goes on there.

Personal blogs

Nyam Penh

nyampenh.com

Nyam Penh is a Phnom Penh blog that does restaurant reviews with lovely photography.

My Big Fat Face

mybigfatface.com

My Big Fat Face is a chronicle of Cambodian food
and parasites.

LTO Cambodia

ltocambodia.blogspot.com

LTO Cambodia contains some amazing stories and
observations by a long-term expat in Cambodia.

Tales From an Expat

talesfromanexpat.com

Tales From an Expat is written by an British man who traded
his 9-to-5 existence for the rice paddies of beautiful Kampot.

Alison in Cambodia

alisonincambodia.wordpress.com

An expat archeologist in Cambodia writes about her work
and archaeological projects, including temple restorations.

Phnom Penh Places

phnompenhplaces.blogspot.com

Phnom Penh Places is a blog documenting the historic
buildings of the city, as well as new developments.

Jobs and classifieds

Bong Thom Classifieds

www.bongthom.com

Bong Thom Classifieds is the biggest classifieds site in
Cambodia and is particularly good for job listings.

Expat Advisory

www.expat-advisory.com/forum/asia/cambodia/
   job-posts-forum-cambodia-all-jobs

Expat Advisory has some job listings aimed at expats.

CamHR

camhr.com

CamHR is a very popular job listing site aimed at
Cambodians, but with some expat-oriented jobs as well.

Top Recruitment

www.top-recruitment.com

Top Recruitment is a leading headhunter in Cambodia.

HR Inc.

www.hrinc.com.kh

HR Inc. is another leading headhunter in Cambodia that
works with expats.

The American Cambodia Business Counci

www.amchamcambodia.net

The American Cambodia Business Council (AmCham)
"serves as the voice of American business within the
Cambodian private sector" and regularly holds networking
events and other activities.

The British Chamber of Commerce Cambodia

www.bbacambodia.com

The British Chamber of Commerce Cambodia holds regular
networking events and activities and is a good business
resource for expats of all nationalities (not just British).

Reliefweb Cambodia

reliefweb.int/country/khm

Reliefweb Cambodia has job postings by the UN in the development sector.

Teaching in Cambodia

Dave's ESL Cafe

forums.eslcafe.com/job/viewforum.php?f=50

Dave's ESL Cafe has a special board for discussion of teaching opportunities in Cambodia.

Khmer440

www.khmer440.com/chat_forum/viewforum.php?f=2

Khmer440 has a board dedicated to discussing the ins and outs of teaching English in Cambodia.

Wandering Educators

www.wanderingeducators.com

Wandering Educators is a global community of educators sharing their travel experiences.

Tefl.com

www.tefl.com/jobs/job.html

Tefl.com occasionally lists good teaching jobs in Cambodia.

Suggested reading

If you're thinking about moving to Cambodia
(or are already here), reading up on the country
will help you gain a better understanding of
its history, its people, and its culture. Here
are some of the best books that are still
widely available.

History

**When the War Was Over: Cambodia and the Khmer Rouge
Revolution** by Elizabeth Becker

Elizabeth Becker was one of only two Western journalists
allowed into Cambodia during the Khmer Rouge era,
and she went on to become one of the leading scholars of
Cambodia's modern history. In *When the War Was Over*,
Becker covers the French colonial period, Cambodian
nationalism, the rise and fall of the Khmer Rouge, all the
way though Pol Pot's death in 1998. Along the way she also
covers other governments' reactions and acquiescence to
the Khmer Rouge's crimes. A wonderful, well-researched
book.

**Cambodia's Curse: The Modern History of a Troubled
Land** by Joel Brinkley

In *Cambodia's Curse*, Pulitzer Prize–winning journalist
Joel Brinkley writes about Cambodia's modern history and
the problems that Cambodia faces a generation after the
Khmer Rouge. The book covers the culture of corruption

in Cambodia (which is nothing new, Brinkley claims), the UN protectorate debacle, Cambodia's powerful dictator, Hun Sen, and exactly how NGOs are destroying the fragile country. Although widely criticized for its bleak outlook, *Cambodia's Curse* is recommended reading for every grumpy expat who worries that he may be alone in his frustration with the Kingdom of Wonder.

The History of Cambodia by David Chandler

Probably the best record of Cambodian history around. In *The History of Cambodia* David Chandler manages to cover the entire history of the country in less than 400 very interesting pages. The book was revised in 2007 to include recent research, more information about the Khmer Rouge period, and a section on the challenges facing Cambodia today. Although pricey, the book is well worth it. If you read only one book about Cambodia, this is a good choice.

Pol Pot: Anatomy of a Nightmare by Philip Short

Considered the definitive portrait of the man who masterminded the takeover of the country that resulted in the deaths of up to 25 percent of its population, *Pol Pot: Anatomy of a Nightmare* is a well-researched, well-written book that gives a chilling depiction of the leader of the Khmer Rouge.

A Record of Cambodia: The Land and Its People by Zhou Daguan

Originally published as *The Customs of Cambodia*, this is a newly updated version of Zhou Daguan's record of nearly a year spent in Cambodia from late 1296 to 1297. Zhou, a

Chinese diplomat, provides one of the only written records from that time of the city of Angkor and the Khmer Empire. Although quite short, the book has enough spicy stuff to make it a worthwhile read, including the declaration that monks were responsible for deflowering Cambodian teenagers. *A Record of Cambodia: The Land and Its People* is Peter Harris' translation of Zhou's records, and the first direct Chinese-to-English translation. (Prior versions had been translated to French before being rendered in English, and many details were lost along the way.) Well worth a read.

Language and culture

Cambodian for Beginners by Richard Gilbert

If you're planning on learning the Khmer language, *Cambodian for Beginners* (with its accompanying CDs) is one of the most complete resources available. In addition to offering an introduction to the spoken language, it also covers Khmer script.

Carrying Cambodia by Hans Kemp and Conor Wall

This collection of photographs captures one of the things that tickles expats the most—the ingenuity that Cambodians deploy to transport things from one place to another. Whether it's a moto stacked with giant live pigs or the back of a truck filled with garment factory workers, *Carrying Cambodia* is a lovely visual depiction of a country in the midst of major change. Makes a great gift for those who may not yet understand your Cambodia obsession, because after this, they will.

Culture Shock! Cambodia: A Survival Guide to Customs and Etiquette by Peter North

In *Culture Shock! Cambodia,* author Peter North gives a good record of the history of Cambodia. His explanations of Cambodian customs are dated, though, and often specifics are lacking.

Food and travel

From Spiders to Water Lilies: Creative Cambodian Cooking with Friends

Local child protection organization Friends International released its second cookbook, *From Spiders to Water Lilies: Creative Cambodian Cooking with Friends,* to much critical acclaim—it's won a couple of awards and is one of the best Cambodian cookbooks currently available. The book contains 34 recipes in English and Khmer, plus pages and pages of lovely photos. The book is more easily available in Cambodia, so wait until you arrive to purchase it.

Lonely Planet Cambodia by Nick Ray and Greg Bloom

Luckily for us, the Cambodian edition is one of the best researched and most thorough Lonely Planets around. Nick Ray and Greg Bloom have done a great job with the 2012 edition, which covers the best accommodations, dining, and activities around the entire country. As with the previous edition, the book contains a thorough guide to the temples of Angkor, but the section on the islands and southern coast is entirely new. A necessary reference for anyone who plans to travel around Cambodia.

RESOURCES

Cambodian Cooking by Joannès Rivière

If you're interested in learning to cook Cambodian food, Joannes Riviere's cookbook is a good place to start. The photographs by Maja Smend are some of the most beautiful depictions of Cambodian food around and will inspire you to learn to cook some Cambodian favorites. Considered one of the foremost authorities on Cambodian food, Riviere is the chef at what is arguably the country's best restaurant, Cuisine Wat Damnak in Siem Reap.

Fiction and memoir

The Disappeared by Kim Echlin

While there are many memoirs and other nonfiction books about Cambodia, very few fictional works are set here, and even fewer love stories. *The Disappeared* by Kim Echlin is a cross-cultural love story about a young Canadian woman, Anne, who falls in love with a Cambodian, Serey, who is trapped in Montreal in the late 1970s because the Khmer Rouge have closed Cambodia's borders. After the Vietnamese invasion he returns to Cambodia, and Anne doesn't hear from him again. Eleven years later Anne thinks she sees Serey on a news report about Cambodia, and she immediately leaves for Phnom Penh to find him. Set against the backdrop of Cambodia's political turmoil, the novel shows these characters wrestling with the ghosts of the past and discovering whether their love can overcome Cambodia's pain.

First They Killed My Father: A Daughter of Cambodia Remembers by Loung Ung

Loung Ung was a privileged Khmer child growing up in Phnom Penh when the Khmer Rouge took power in 1975. *First They Killed My Father* is her memoir of life under the Khmer Rouge, from being forcibly evacuated from Phnom Penh at the age of five to serving as a child soldier and losing many members of her family. *First They Killed My Father* is written from the author's perspective as a child, and the book is easily one of the most accessible narratives of the period. A good introductory book for those who want to better understand the horrors of the Khmer Rouge without cracking open a history textbook.

About the author

Lina Goldberg is a freelance writer based in Phnom Penh, Cambodia, who specializes in food, travel, and culture. She has contributed to publications including Lonely Planet, CNN Travel, *South China Morning Post*, Vice, and BBC Travel.

Before moving to Cambodia, Lina worked at Google in the United States, Ireland, and the United Kingdom. She originally came to Cambodia on a three-month fellowship with a backpack and little else. She immediately fell in love with the country and two years later, she's still here.

About Imaginary Shapes

Imaginary Shapes is Frances Duncan and Dan O. Williams. They specialize in the planning, art direction, and design of ebook ecosystems. They are based in the Berkshires of western Massachusetts.

www.movetocambodia.com

For more about moving to and living in Cambodia, including our regularly updated blog about what's happening in the Kingdom of Wonder, visit us at www.movetocambodia.com.

Made in the USA
Lexington, KY
01 October 2014